Drugs Law

W.T. West,

LL.B, Solicitor

Chichester
Barry Rose Publishers Ltd
1982

© 1982 W.T. West

ISBN   0-85992-228-6

Published by
Barry Rose Pulishers Ltd.
Little London, Chichester
West Sussex. PO19 1PG.
Printed by
Commercial Print Service
Portsmouth, England

DRUGS LAW

ACKNOWLEDGMENTS

The author acknowledges his debt to HMSO for their gallant attempts to supply the Acts and statutory instruments needed, during an industrial dispute, for the writing of much of this short introduction to a branch of the criminal law which, due to what may be broadly termed the pro-cannabis and anti-cannabis lobby, is of no small importance to judges, lawyers, police officers, doctors, hospitals, social workers, and dentists.

He further acknowledges his debt to various secondary sources. These include inter alia:-

1. The Pharmaceutical Press.
2. Gaddon's Pharmacopia.
3. Halsbury's Statutes, both old and modern editions.
4. Dick Lee and Colin Pratt's "Operation Julie" (W.H. Allen).
5. Graham's "Cannabis Now".
6. Stone's Justices' Manual.
7. The Law Society's Gazette (Various articles).
8. Dale and Appelbe's "Pharmacy Law and Ethics". (1976).

The law is stated (to the best of this author's knowledge and belief) as at August 19, 1981. The author thanks his wife for not introducing misspellings. Any errors are his own.

CONTENTS

TABLES OF STATUTES

AND OF INTERNATIONAL LAW

INTERNATIONAL CONVENTIONS ETC

TABLE OF RULES AND REGULATIONS

TABLE OF CASES

"Sherlock Holmes thrust the sharp point home, pressed down the tiny piston and sank back into the armchair with a sigh of satisfaction. 'Which is it today', I asked, 'morphine or cocaine?' 'It is cocaine', he said, 'a seven per cent solution. Would you care to try it?' 'No, indeed', I answered. brusquely.'" (*The Sign of Four*, A. Conan Doyle, 1890.)

Before the Great War, a citizen had remarkable freedom. He could live as and when he wished. He had no driving licence, insurance certificate or identity card. He could go overseas without a passport or official permission. He could change sterling into other currency without limit or restriction. If an alien, he could live here without leave to enter the country, and need not register with the police. He could enter an opium den. He could purchase and use dangerous drugs. Sir Arthur Conan Doyle in no way tarnished his hero's reputation in the eyes of any reader, young or old, by revealing his drug addiction and there was no law against it.

In 1912, an International Convention was held to discuss control of traffic in opium, and Indian hemp. There was an Opium Conference in 1924. The League of Nations set up a Committee on traffic in opium and dangerous drugs. As a continuation, after the Second World War, the United Nations appointed a commission on narcotics drugs. An International Narcotics Control Board came into existence. The World Health Organisation was established at Geneva. In 1961, Britain became a party to a Convention which came into force in 1964, mainly concerned with opium and its derivatives. A standing Advisory Committee on the misuse of drugs set up in 1966 has considered, inter alia, cannabis. The Wootton Report was produced in 1967 and the Deedes Report in 1970. The first Act of Parliament on the subject was the Dangerous Drugs Act 1920, and the principal Act now governing the position is the Misuse of Drugs Act 1971. It divides drugs into Class A drugs and Class B drugs, offences in relation to the former attracting greater penalties and it superseded the Dangerous Drugs Act 1965, and the Drugs (Prevention of Misuse) Act 1964.

Today, therefore, Sherlock Holmes might possibly have been the concern of the Central Drugs Intelligence Unit, on the fourth floor of Scotland Yard, or one of the many police drug squads coping with illicit sales of dangerous drugs and the misuse of drugs generally — unless he could have persuaded Dr. Watson to prescribe for his addiction, when he could lawfully have been supplied with any narcotic of his choice. The drugs which are perhaps of most interest to those squads are lysergic acid diethylamide, cannabis, cocaine, heroin and morphine.

Lysergic acid diethylamide (LSD) is regarded by many as being the most dangerous. It has been and is the subject of much controversy. It is a synthetic hallucinogen. The base material is ergotamine tartrate. This is mainly produced in Czechoslovakia. LSD is manufactured in crystal or liquid form. The crystals appear like fine grains of sand and the liquid has neither colour nor smell. If a dose is visible, then it is a large overdose and likely to prove fatal to the taker of it. It can be injected or swallowed. After a time the reaction begins — the quantity taken and the subject's reaction being the relevant factors. It was discovered in 1938 by a scientist named Hoffman who was looking for a drug to alleviate his migraine. His tests were inconclusive but he resumed them in 1943. He accidentally took a dose himself and its effect caused him to continue researching. In 1947 he made his discoveries public. They sparked off interest and controversy in the medical and scientific world and volunteers came forward to take the drug under supervision. Unlike opiates, such as morphine, heroin and opium, which induce physical dependence, that is physical illness if the drug is withheld, LSD, like amphetamine, cocaine and cannabis, induces only emotional dependence — that is, emotional distress if the drug is withheld. The controversy about LSD arises from the clash between those doctors, a minority, who think it is of assistance on the treatment of mental illness and others, the majority who consider it to be physically dangerous and capable of permanently damaging the personality. The physical reaction when LSD is taken may be simply a quickening or slowing of the pulse, or a decrease or increase of the blood pressure, or blurred vision. But the mental reactions will affect all the senses. If used in chemical warfare, LSD could possibly knock out a whole nation. Two attache cases of LSD, put into the water supply, would, it has been conjectured, incapacitate the United States for many hours. It has been used for more laudable purposes by doctors, for example, to relieve the pain and despair of cancer sufferers, or to cure alcoholics. Dealing in LSD brings large profits to the law-breakers and it is very difficult to detect. Young persons have died, or had their lives irretrievably damaged by taking LSD.

Cannabis is even more controversial and more has been written about this than about any other drug. It has been illegal here for many years and it is thought that at least five million people have used it. Since 1965, more than five thousand people have been imprisoned for possessing it, and there have been nearly 90,000 convictions for cannabis offences. Cannabis (sometimes called hemp) is a green plant which can grow as high as 15 feet, although in the United Kingdom it seldom passes the five feet mark. It was first cultivated in China. There is a reference to it in the writings of Herodotus about 500 B.C. It was probably brought to Europe by the Crusaders. Napoleon is known to have disapproved of it, and to have promulgated a decree banning its use. Today that use is world-wide. The plant is an annual, it grows quickly, and has a woody, hairy stem. The leaves are borne on a long stalk and are sub-divided into leaflets. There are small flowers. The ovary is a single seed enclosed in a bract covered in hairs, and the glands which secrete the resin are at the base of the hair. Herbal cannabis or the leaf is called marijuana or "pot", and the resin is termed hashish. The material which affects the mind is called tetrahydro-cannabinsh (THC). There is more of this to be found in the resin of a plant than in the leaf.

Cultivated first as a food plant and a source of fibre, it soon achieved a reputation as an intoxicant. What is the effect of cannabis on the mind? There appears to be a feeling of elevation of the spirits. Smokers of cannabis claim to experience no ill effects on the following day. The pleasant effect lasts from six to eight hours and is followed by drowsiness or sleep. The smoking of cannabis is obviously likely to affect the subject's ability to drive a motor vehicle and it is an offence to be in charge of one while under the influence of a drug to such an extent as to be incapable of proper control (Road Traffic Act 1972, s.5). Cannabis may change intellectual ability, but only in its short term effects. Experts do not consider there is any association between violence and cannabis. The popular method of using cannabis is to inhale it by smoking a cigarette popularly termed a "reefer". Herbal cannabis (marijuana or pot) (the leaf) or cannabis resin (hashish) is rolled with tobacco.

The resin is made into a cake, which can be cut with a knife. In recent years, cannabis oil has come on to the market. It is extracted from a cake of resin. The THC in cannabis oil may be as high as 50 or 60 per cent. The oil is dribbled onto the surface of a cigarette. When THC enters the lungs in smoke it is carried off by the blood, then it leaves the blood and penetrates the brain, where it exerts the effect sought by the smoker. There is in the United Kingdom a pro-cannabis and an anti-cannabis group. The former direct their attack at s.52 of the Criminal Law Act 1977, which outlawed cannabis leaves, reversing the decision of the House of Lords in *R. v Goodchild* [1978] 1 WLR 578. The United Kingdom is party to the United Nations Single Convention, 1961, which specifically excludes leaves, so that the 1977 Act has created a state of affairs in which cannabis is controlled more stringently than in most other countries. Convictions for cannabis offences average over 10,000 per annum. It would appear, from the magazine *Police,* that the obligation to enforce our cannabis law may have sadly exacerbated relations between young persons and the police. The National Council for Civil Liberties, who regularly campaign in their journal *Rights* for the law to be changed as does also the Legalize Cannabis Campaign, express the view that cannabis is a harmless drug, no more than a mild intoxicant. The other group — James Callaghan is a supporter of it, and in 1969 urged the House of Commons "to call a halt in the advancing tide of so-called permissiveness" — takes a rather different view, and concentrate on the facts that hallucinations may be caused by large doses of cannabis, that there is frequently a loss of appreciation of space and time, and that changes occur in the catecholamine content of the brain. Possibly the real danger is thought to be that the smoker of cannabis will wish to proceed to use more dangerous drugs.

Cocaine is a local anaesthetic. It acts on the nervous system. It has its own advenergic action. It produces stimulation of the higher centres of the brain, resulting in restlessness, then depression, and it is a drug of addiction. Victims who increase their intake may lose all self-control, develop tremors, and become melancholic or even insane. Large doses may produce convulsions followed by paralysis. The coca bush, growing wild in South America, contains cocaine — an alkaloid. Taking cocaine produces a racing heart and high blood pressure. It can be taken in the "pure" form, or as cocaine-hydrochloride — in the latter form it is most easily assimilable. The maximum daily dose on record, the patient surviving, is said to be 150 milligrams. Addicts may have the ability to work for days without sufficient sleep, or rest, but suffer sharp changes of mood, and many collapse into somnolence or coma. Doctors nowadays do not inject cocaine. It is applied to the surface of the body. It may be sniffed in the form of a powder. Addicts have been known to mix it with heroin. Like opium, morphine, heroin etc., cocaine is controlled by law in all countries. In a clever essay published in America the psychiatrist, Dr. David Musto, plausibly connected Conan Doyle's detective with Dr. Sigmund Freud, the Austrian doctor, by the link of cocaine.

Heroin induces severe physical dependence and there is physical illness if the drug is withheld. It is a central nervous system depressant. More powerful than morphine, it has fewer side-effects. It is used by the medical profession to relieve severe pain, usually in a terminal illness. Its use is controlled by law in virtually every country, and there is a big international traffic in it. An overdose can prove fatal, as the subject's breathing fails. It is short acting, and usually has to be injected. If the equipment is not steri-lized, local ulcers, possibly a liver disease called hepatitis or even death results. The heroin addict is often a socially inadequate person, who cannot keep a job. Heroin may be prescribed by a doctor, in his discretion, for the treatment of a disease as also in cases of registered addiction. Heroin is produced by a modification of morphine, quite easily effected.

Morphine is a drug of addiction and patients become dependent on it. Pharmacologically, it has a resemblance to cannabis. Morphine can be swallowed, injected or smoked. The effect begins in approximately half an hour, does not start to pass away until three to five hours have elapsed and may last 12 hours. It exerts an effect on the central nervous system, causing depression and excitation of certain areas. It produces reduction of the emotions and powers of anxiety, concentration and fear. Pain is reduced and a feeling of con-tentment ensues. The respiratory centre and the cough centre are depressed and a large dose will kill. There is a feeling of heaviness in the limbs, itching, a dry mouth and reduced hunger. It causes retention of both bile and urine. Tolerance to it occurs and over a period the dose taken has to be increased if it is to produce the same effect. Pethedine, methadone and codeine are well-known morphine-like compounds.

In Britain, except in the case of cannabis, the control of dangerous drugs is efficient. In the free and easy days prior to August 1914, drug addicts were not regarded, by the law or by themselves, as criminals or "drop-outs". Madeline Smith bought her arsenic, R. L. Stevenson bought his laudanum. It was as simple as going to the off-licence for a crate of beer today. No social suspicion, no social ostracism, resulted. A popular prejudice began to grow after the turn of the century. It came to be realized that, in general, the constant taking of dangerous drugs (often referred to by both addicts and police officers as "dope") had a harmful effect on the general health, and it was wrong to take certain drugs except for remedial purposes and on medical advice. The common drugs of addiction, in addition to those already described, are amphetamine (not dissimilar from THC in action, but not mutual antagonists), opium (the dried juice from capsules of the opium poppy, an age-old narcotic, emanating from or originating in the Far East, now extensively cultivated in Thailand, Burmah and Turkey), dilandid, metopon, pikeridime, levorphan, and the stereoisomeric forms and salts of these substances.

As a result of a report of the Advisory Committee on Drug Dependence in 1968, probation officers were encouraged to play a positive role in the rehabilitaton of drug addicts.

II

The initial reaction of Parliament towards drugs was to put a tax on them. Thus, under the Medicines Stamp Act 1802, it was enacted that no person might take advantage of, or make, compound, or utter, sell, or expose for sale any drugs which were subject to duty, unless he obtained a licence. The licence duty was five shillings per annum. Duties on packets, boxes and phials containing any drugs were prescribed by the Stamp Act 1804, on an ad valorem scale, according to the price or value. By the Medicines Stamp Act 1812, drugs mentioned in Sir Harbottle Grimstone's Book of Rates, *i.e.* special drugs and also unmixed drugs sold by surgeons, chemists or druggists, were exempted. But until 1920, the right to sell drugs, other than poisons, was not affected by the statutes dealing with chemists and druggists. In the criminal law, it was made an offence, by s.22 of the Offences Against the Person Act 1861, to apply or administer any stupefying or overpowering drug with intent to commit any indictable offence, the maximum punishment being penal servitude for life. It was also provided by s.23 of the same Act, that an offence was committed by a person who unlawfully and maliciously caused another to take a noxious thing so as to endanger life. In an interesting, if perhaps a trifle irrelevant, recent case on s.23, namely *R. v. Cato, R. v. Morris, R. v. Dudley (CA)* [1975] 119 SJ 775, an appeal by the defendants was dismissed. It was held, that the injection of another person with morphine which a defendant has unlawfully taken into his possession, is an unlawful act, and if death results, the offence committed is manslaughter. This is the case, even if the injection was not necessarily the only or the major cause of the death resulting. Furthermore, the court held that both heroin (otherwise called diamorphine) and morphine are "noxious things" within the meaning of s.23 of the Offences Against the Person Act 1861, and also held that the requirement of malice (a term which of course connotes intention or recklessness, and is not synonymous with "wickedly") in that section was satisfied where the act done to the victim was a direct one, such as an injection.

The Dangerous Drugs Act 1920, and later statutes, were passed partly as a result of domestic legislative pressures, and partly international action, since smuggling jeopardizes any control purely national in its scope. Various international conventions and agreements were made, namely the Shanghai Agreement of 1909, the Hague Convention of 1912, the Geneva Second Opium Convention of 1925, the Convention for Limiting the Manufacture and Regulating the Distribution of Narcotic Drugs of 1931, the Covention for Suppression of the Illicit Traffic in Dangerous Drugs (Geneva 1936), and finally the 1948 protocol and the opium protocol of 1953. The codification of all above mentioned treaties and agreements into a single convention was agreed in New York in 1961, the convention to come into force when forty States had deposited instruments of ratification.

The Dangerous Drugs Act 1951, consolidated with amendment the Dangerous Drugs Acts 1920 to 1950, *i.e.* the Dangerous Drugs Act 1920, the Dangerous Drugs and Poisons (Amendment) Act 1923, the Dangerous Drugs Act 1925, the Dangerous Drugs Act 1932, and the Dangerous Drugs (Amendment) Act 1950. There was little case law, perhaps a tribute to the care taken in drafting the legislation, or more probably, due to the absence of a drug problem of any size, but mention may be made of *R. v. Yasukichi Miyaguwa* [1924] 1 K.B. 614, when it was held that the accused was properly convicted of "procuring" (within the meaning of regulations made under s.7 of the Dangerous Drugs Act 1920) morphine by ordering the drugs in Switzerland for dispatch to Japan, the bills of lading and other shipping documents being received in London.

The 1951 Act was in five parts. Part I (ss. 1-4) dealt with raw opium, coca leaves, Indian hemp and its resins which were not to be imported or exported without licence. Part II (ss. 5-7) prohibited the import or export of opium prepared for smoking and made it an offence to make, have in possession, smoke, allow on premises for smoking, *etc.*, any such opium. Part III (ss. 8-10) provided for regulations to control manufacture, sale, use, *etc.*, of medicinal opium, extract of Indian hemp, morphine, cocaine, *etc.* Part V (ss. 13-26) — s.14 enacted that a constable or person authorized by the Secretary of State might enter the premises of a person dealing in the above drugs and inspect books and stocks of any such drugs and a justice, on sworn information, might issue a search warrant authorizing entry of premises, search and seizure of any such drugs and documents relating to the same. Any delay or obstruction was an offence. Under s.15, breaches of regulations or licences or false statements or aiding *etc.* same were made offences punishable summarily or (if the Attorney-General or the Director of Public Prosecutions gave his consent) on indictment. By s.18, summary proceedings had to be taken within three months from the date when a Secretary of State gave a certificate that there was evidence sufficient for a prosecution. Section 19 enacted that a constable might arrest without warrant a person who had committed or attempted to commit any offence against the Act or Regulations made thereunder, if the officer had reasonable grounds for believing that the person would abscond unless arrested or if his name and address were unknown and could not be ascertained.

The Dangerous Drugs Regulations 1953, made under the Act, entitled doctors, pharmacists, *etc.* to supply the drugs in Part I of the Act. As to the drugs in Part III of the Act, the manufacture, supply *etc.* of them was prohibited except by authorized persons. A similar exemption for drugs in Part III of the Act was enjoyed by doctors, pharmacists, *etc.* The master of a ship without a doctor was allowed to have the necessary drugs. Farmers or stock owners with police certificates might hold limited quantity of opium. Certified midwives might have medicinal opium and pethidine, to be kept locked up. There were restrictions on the manufacture of codeine and other drugs. Registers and records, except national health prescriptions, had to be preserved for two years.

III

The modern legislation really begins with the Dangerous Drugs Act 1964, and the Drugs (Prevention of Misuse) Act 1964 — the former Act introduced wholly new offences concerning cannabis and the cannabis plant, and consists of 11 sections and 2 schedules. Section 8 of the 1951 Act had restricted the importation and exportation of the drugs in Part III. A new list of drugs was now substituted — the drugs listed in Part I of sch. 1 to the 1964 Act, other than preparations within part II of the schedule, the latter consisting of preparations with no, or a negligible, risk of abuse, or not constituting a risk to health, containing not more than 100 milligrammes of the substance per dosage unit. The drugs in Part I of the new schedule included any extract or tincture of cannabis. Schedule 1 could be modified by Order in Council following any new decision of the Commission on Narcotic Drugs of the United Nations. Part I of the 1951 Act had restricted the importation of raw opium, coca leaves, Indian hemp and resins obtained therefrom, except under licence and into an approved port. All ports were now to be alike, the requirements of use of approved ports being abolished, and poppy-straw (*i.e.* all parts except the seeds of the opium poppy), cannabis and cannabis resin were substituted for Indian hemp and its resins. The new offences formed the subject of ss. 9 and 10. It was enacted that if a person being the occupier of any premises permitted those premises to be used for smoking cannabis or cannabis resin, or was concerned in the management of any premises used for any such purpose, an offence was committed. Further, a person who, except under Home Office licence, knowingly cultivated a cannabis plant, was guilty of an offence. "Cannabis" (except when used in the expression "cannabis resin") was defined as "the flowering or fruiting tops of any plant of the genus cannabis from which the resin had not been extracted". "Cannabis resin" was to mean the separated resin, whether crude or purified obtained from any cannabis plant. The drafting of these sections were to give lawyers and judges much cause for thought.

The appellant in *Sweet v. Parsley* [1970] AC 132, was a Miss Stephanie Sweet, a schoolmistress. She taught at a school in Oxford. She was convicted by the justices on September 14, 1967 on a charge that on June 16, 1967, she was concerned in the management of certain premises at a farm in Oxfordshire which were used for smoking cannabis. Having been fined she appealed. The tenant of the farm sublet the farmhouse to Miss Sweet at a rent of £28 per four weeks. What she wanted to do was to live in the house and travel daily to her school by car. This proved impracticable so she resided in Oxford when she was teaching. She let rooms in the house at low rents to tenants, allowing them the common use of the kitchen. She kept one room for her own use. She visited the farm occasionally to collect her letters, to collect rent from her tenants and generally to see that all was well. Sometimes she stayed overnight, but generally she did not. On June 16, 1967, while Miss Sweet was at Oxford, the police went to the premises with a search warrant. They found receptacles in the garden which contained cannabis resin and LSD. They found, in the kitchen, cigarette ends containing cannabis and an ornamental hookah pipe which was Miss Sweet's and had, without her knowledge, been used for smoking this substance. The justices found that at the time of the search Miss Sweet was not at the premises but there was a mixture of people there of the 'beatnik' fraternity between the ages of 17 and 22. Miss Sweet's conviction was quashed by the House of Lords. When s.9 of the 1964 Act, which by this time had become s.5 of the Dangerous Drugs Act 1965, used the words "used for any such purpose", was the "purpose" the purpose of the smoker or the purpose of the management? The purpose was, said Lord Reid, the purpose of the management. It would be a strange use of language to say that a room was "used for the purpose" of smoking cannabis when all that happened was that some visitor lighted a cannabis cigarette there.

Later in the same year, the Drugs (Prevention of Misuse) Act 1964 was passed to penalize the possession and restrict the importation of drugs of certain kinds not previously outlawed. It left the Dangerous Drugs Acts 1951 and 1964, untouched, constituting a special code on its own. Section 1 provided that subject to exemptions, it should not be lawful for a person to have in his possession a substance for the time being specified in the Schedule to the Act, unless it was in his possession by a doctor's or dentist's prescription, or the person was a registered manufacturer or dealer. There was of course the usual exemption for doctors, dentists, veterinary practitioners, chemists, authorised sellers of poisons, public analysts, owners of medical store — carrying ships, constables *etc*. The drugs specified in the Schedule were aminopropylbenzene, aminoisopropylbenzene, chlorphentermine, permoline and synthetic compounds from and salts of these substances. By s.2, a constable might arrest without warrant a person found committing, or reasonably suspected of committing, an offence, if the constable had reasonable grounds for believing that that person would abscond unless arrested, or the name and address of the person were unknown and could not be ascertained, or the constable was suspicious that a false name and address had been given. By s.3 if a justice was satisfied there was reasonable ground for suspecting that any of the four drugs was in the possession of a person in any premises, he could issue a search warrant to enter the premises and to search for and seize the drugs. By s.5, the importation, except under Home Office licence, of the four drugs was prohibited.

An elementary error or omission in the drafting of s.1 led to *R. v. Warner* [1969] AC 256. Mr. Warner was charged with having drugs in his possession without authority contrary to s.1. A police officer stopped him when he was driving a van in the back of which were found three cases, one of which contained scent bottles and another, a plastic bag, contained 20,000 amphetamine sulphate tablets. Mr. Warner had been to a café where he was accustomed to collect scent. He was told by the proprietor that a parcel was under the counter. He found two parcels there, one containing scent and the other which was found to contain the drug. He said he had assumed that both contained scent. Section 1 did not define "possession". Warner's case became and is a leading case on the meaning of the word, and was followed in *R. v. Ashton-Rickhardt* [1978] 1 WLR 37. It was the first case in which the House of Lords considered whether a statutory offence was an absolute offence in the sense that the belief, intention or state of mind of the accused was immaterial and irrelevant and the decision went against Mr. Warner. Lord Morris said that a start must be made with the literal meaning. "Possession" involved in the first place that you knew you had something in your possession; it did not involve that you knew precisely what it was that you had got. "In a case like this", said Lord Morris, "it is for the prosecution to establish (a) that the accused was knowingly in control of some article or thing or substance or package or container in circumstances which had enabled him to know or discover what it was that he had before assuming control of it or continuing to be in control of it, and (b) whether the accused knew this or not, the article or thing or substance or package or container that he had consisted of or contained a prohibited substance". It was the declared purpose of the Act to prevent the misuse of drugs and, save in the case of the persons exempted, *e.g.* doctors, Parliament had apparently decided to forbid possession absolutely.

The Dangerous Drugs Act 1965, consolidated the Dangerous Drugs Acts 1951 and 1964. Section 13, repeating s.13 of the Dangerous Drugs Act 1920, and s.15 of the Dangerous Drugs Act 1951, enacted that a person who in the United Kingdom aided, abetted, counselled or procured the commisssion in a place outside the United Kingdom of an offence punishable under the provisions of a "corresponding law" in force in that place, or did an act preparatory to, or in furtherance of, an act which if committed in the U.K. would constitute an offence against the 1965 Act, was guilty of an offence. Professional smugglers are clever, and this country is sometimes a transit stage. Drugs are re-exported to America and the Commonwealth. A simple ruse is to despatch parcels, by post, to accommodation addresses where the parcels are altered, and the country of origin is hidden in this way. It is the person receiving the package, not the organiser, who is liable to arrest. There are unlawful landings from boats, and drugs are concealed in hidden compartments of vehicles making long overland journeys. "Corresponding law" in s.13 was defined by s.23 as "a law stated in a certificate purporting to be issued by or on behalf of the government of a country outside the U.K. to be a law providing for the control and regulation in that country of the manufacture, sale, use, export and import of drugs and other substances in accordance with the provisions of the Single Convention or a law providing for the control and regulation in that country of the manufacture, sale, use, export and import of drugs in accordance with the provisions of the Hague Convention, the Geneva Convention (No. 1) and the Geneva Convention (No. 2) as respectively amended by the Protocol." A statement in any such certificate was to be conclusive as to the effect of the law mentioned in the certificate. A statement in any such certificate that any facts constituted an offence was to be conclusive also.

The Dangerous Drugs Act 1967 was passed to provide for the control of drug addiction. By s.1, the Home Office took power to make regulations requiring any medical practitioner attending a drug addict to furnish particulars to the authorities, and prohibiting any medical practitioner from administering, supplying and prescribing drugs of specified kinds for drug addicts except under licence. Contravention of the regulations could lead to a direction prohibiting the practitioner from administering *etc.* the drugs specified in that direction. Tribunals were constituted to investigate contraventions of the regulations. They could make recommendations whereupon notice in writing had to be served on the doctor, who could make representations. The Home Secretary was then under a duty to refer the representations to an advisory body. The final result could be a direction as mentioned, or an order referring the case back to the tribunal, or an order that no further proceedings be taken. Section 4 was of importance to doctors, chemists, hospitals *etc.* It empowered the Home Office to make regulations requiring precautions to be taken for the safe custody of drugs, requiring the keeping of records, containing provision for the inspection of precautions taken or records kept, and prescribing the manner in which drugs were to be packed for sale by manufacturers or dealers.

The regulations were to provide for the case of a person referred to in s.1(2) of the Drugs (Prevention of Misuse) Act 1964, being convicted of an offence against the 1965 Act, for example the case of a doctor leaving drugs in his car, a chemist not keeping records, or a manufacturer carelessly packing drugs for sale. Such a conviction might lead to a direction prohibiting the offender from having possession of drugs specified in the 1964 Act. Extensive further powers to make regulations were given to the Home Secretary. The power of arrest conferred on constables by s.2 of the Drugs (Prevention of Misuse) Act 1964, had been confined to persons in unauthorised possession of the drugs specified in the Act, and the powers of search were similarly restricted. Additional powers of search were now given to constables. By s.6, if a constable had reasonable grounds for suspecting a person to be in possession of a drug in contravention of the 1964 or 1965 Acts or regulations, he might search the person, detain him for search, search a vehicle, stop a vehicle for that purpose and seize and detain anything found as evidence. These powers were additional to those already exercisable. Clinics were now set up to prescribe for addicts. They were generally out-patient departments at hospitals.

The Report of the Wootton Committee was produced in 1968. They stated (para. 87) that in considering the scale of current penalties for possession of cannabis, their main aim, having regard to their view of the known effects of cannabis, was to remove for practical purposes the prospect of imprisonment for possession of a small amount and to demonstrate that taking the drug in moderation was a relatively minor offence. Backed by the whole Committee, this aim was rejected by the politicians and the courts. In 1975, for example, the number of persons dealt with on charges of posssession of cannabis, *etc.*, was 7,221. 6,744 were convicted. Of these, 4,893 were fined, and 372 were given a custodial sentence, *i.e.* prison, borstal, detention centre or community home.

In the field of statutory instruments the Dangerous Drugs Regulations 1952, mentioned at page 9, had by this time vanished. In their place was the D.D.A. 1965 (Modification) Order 1965, the D.D.A. 1965 (Modification Order 1966, the D.D.A. (Modification No. 2) Order 1966, the D.D.A. 1965 (Modification) Order 1967, the D.D.A. 1965 (Modification) Order 1968, the D.D.A. (Modification) Order 1969, the D.D. (Approved Institutions) Order and the D.D. (No. 2) Regulations 1964, the D.D. Regulations 1965, the D.D. (Notification of Addicts) Regulations 1968, and the D.D. (Supply to Addicts) Regulations 1968. (The last two were revoked by SI 1973/799). Overlapping, as it were, with poisons law, were the D. (Prevention of Misuse) Exemptions Regulations 1964, and the D. (Prevention of Misuse) Modification Order 1966. Lysergide (LSD) was a poison included in the Fourth Schedule to the Poisons Rules, as well as a substance set out in the D. (Prevention of Misuse) Act Schedule as amended by the D. (Prevention of Misuse) Act 1964 Modification Orders. Finally came the Dangerous Drugs (Amendment) Regulations 1970, and the Drugs (Prevention of Misuse) Act 1964, Modification Order 1978, under which possession of amphetamine, cannabinol and its tetrahydro derivatives, lysergamide, pemoline, and many other drugs were declared unlawful.

IV

Having produced three Acts in four years, Parliament subsided until 1971. It fell to the courts to construe the language of the Acts. The following decisions, unlike some already mentioned, remain reliable in the interpretation of the modern legislation.

In *R. v. Harris* [1968] 2 All E.R. 49, the meaning of the word "supply" was the issue. A man was passing the waiting room at a station. He saw the appellant and a man named Fowler sitting close together. Sticking in Fowler's arm was a syringe. A constable was called and saw the appellant, a registered drug addict, injecting Fowler's arm. She was convicted of "supplying" a dangerous drug (heroin) to Fowler. Her appeal was allowed. "The prosecution's case", said Lord Parker, C.J., "is that if A injects B with B's heroin, A is supplying heroin. The court is quite unable to accept that proposition".

Hambleton v. Callinan [1968] 2 All E.R. 943, was a case on unauthorised "possession". The respondents were held to be in possession of traces of amphetamine powder found in samples of their urine. It was, said the court, a wholly artifical conception to contend that a man is in possession of a drug if he has traces of it in his urine or any part of his body in which it can be found. Once one has consumed a drug, and its whole character has been altered, and no further use can be made of it, one is not in possession of it.

In *R. v. Frederick* [1970] 1 W.L.R. 107, there was a charge of unauthorised possession of 307 grains of cannabis resin. A package containing that quantity of cannabis resin was found in a T.V. set in a passage next to the defendant's flat, and a pouch and pipes containing what the analyst called "traces" of cannabis and cannabis resin was found in the flat. The chairman told the jury, and the Court of Appeal upheld him, that the jury could find the defendant guilty of the offence on the possession of "traces" alone. The "traces" were sufficient to constitute the presence of the drug. Possession of the "traces" could be relied on to found the conviction. There was no challenge of the evidence with a view to establishing that what were described as "traces" of cannabis and cannabis resin in the pouch and pipes in reality amounted to nothing.

The next two cases were similar. In *R. v. Worsell* [1970] 1 W.L.R. 111, police officers stopped a car in which the defendant and his co-defendants were driving. The defendant was a passenger. Under the dashboard was a syringe and a small tube. The tube had at one time contained heroin. The defendant's admission made it clear that at some earlier period he was in possession of the drug. Strangely, he was not charged in respect of the earlier period. He was charged with possession of heroin (which, as mentioned, is the better known name of diamorphine) at the moment when the car was stopped. The tube then appeared to be completely empty. There were a very few small droplets impossible to measure and impossible to pour out. The tube was in reality empty. Whatever the tube contained, it could neither be used nor sold. The man was therefore not guilty of unauthorised possession of the drug.

In *R. v. Graham* [1970] 1 W.L.R. 113, the decision went the other way. Graham appealed because he read the *Worsell* case in a paper. He was charged with being in possession of cannabis resin. The police raided his flat, and took some scrapings from his pockets. Traces of cannabis were found in the scrapings. The quantity was capable of being weighed and measured. Since what was found in each of the three pockets could in fact be measured and weighed in milligrammes, the defendant was properly convicted.

R. v. Souter [1971] 2 All E.R. 115 was a case in which a man owned a house and let off rooms. He was charged with permitting premises to be used for the purpose of smoking cannabis. The facts are hardly of interest. The Court of Appeal held that the word "permit" in s.5 of the 1965 Act must be taken to mean actual knowledge that the premises were being used for the purpose of smoking cannabis or knowledge of circumstances such that the person charged could be said to have shut his eyes to the obvious or allowed matters to go on without caring whether or not the smoking of cannabis had been taking place. It was wrong to equate reasonable ground for suspicion with suspicion. It was also wrong to equate suspicion with knowledge.

The word "occupier" was not defined in the enactments, and this brought further employment to the gentlemen of the long robe at the Glamorgan Assize on February 10 and 11, 1970. The case is *R. v. Moglord* [1970] 1 W.L.R. 988. Two sisters, aged 20 and 15, were arraigned on an indictment charging them with permitting premises to be used for the purpose of smoking cannabis. They lived with their parents. While their parents were away on holiday, the police raided the house. As a result both girls faced the charge, and the defence submitted that they could not be the occupiers of their parents' home at a time when their parents were away on holiday. The judge said that the defendants, charged as principals, would only be the occupiers if they were in legal possession of the premises and had control over them. Two requirements were present in the section, first, the defendants must be the occupiers (which they were not, they were the daughters of parents temporarily away on holiday), and secondly, the defendants permitted the premises to be used for the purpose of smoking cannabis. The defendants were acquitted.

In *R. v. Doot* [1972] 116 S.J. 445, the defendants were Americans. They conspired in Belgium or Morocco to import cannabis into the U.K., through England and Canada. They bought the cannabis in Morocco. Then they arrived in England where they were charged with and convicted of conspiring to import dangerous drugs, the particulars of the offence being that they in Hampshire and elsewhere conspired fraudulently to evade the prohibition imposed by the 1965 Act on the importation of cannabis resin into the U.K. They successfully appealed against conviction. The scheme had been agreed outside England. A conspiracy made outside England might be triable in England, but only if an agreement was made in England to work out details for furthering the original agreement. The defendants' acts subsequent to importation merely evidenced the conspiracy.

It has been thought that it would be useful to describe the law on which the repeals made by the Misuse of Drugs Act 1971, operated, and further that the present law is best understood by a brief sketch of the haphazard laws existing before the 1971 Act produced a codified system.

V

The Misuse of Drugs Act 1971 was passed on May 27, 1971, and came into operation on July 1, 1973. The provisions of the Act were criticised at the time, in relation to cannabis, and the severity of the penalties. Section 28, reversing the onus of proof, was criticised, as was the retention of the stop-search powers. Those who praised the purpose of the Act suggested that it did not go far enough — it failed to provide for compulsory detention or hospitalisation of addicts, and it is still no offence to be in a public place, incapable of having proper control of oneself by reason of having taken drugs obtained without a prescription. If, at the start of a police raid, drugs are quickly consumed or destroyed, proof of possession apparently cannot be established.

Section 1 set up an advisory body. It replaced the former Advisory Committee on Drug Dependence. It was termed the "Advisory Council". The Council's duty is to keep under review the situation in the U.K. with respect to drugs which are being, or appear to the Council likely to be, misused, and of which the misuse is having or appears to the Council capable of having, harmful effects sufficient to constitute a social problem, and to give the Ministers advice on measures, whether or not involving alteration of the law, which in the opinion of the Council ought to be taken for preventing the misuse of drugs or dealing with social problems connected with their misuse. In particular advice is tendered on the measures to be taken to restrict the availability of drugs, or supervisory arrangements for their supply, for enabling persons affected by misuse to obtain advice, for securing the provision of proper facilities and services for the treatment, rehabilitation and after-care of such persons, for educating the public, and especially the young, in the dangers of misuse of drugs, and for promoting research into matters of relevance for preventing misuse. The Council also considers and advises the Home Office on communications received from any authority established under a treaty or convention to which the country is a party. By ss. 2 and 7 the Advisory Council must first be consulted by the Home Department, before Orders in Council are made adding drugs to the list of those controlled or removing them, and before a designation order is made under s.7(4).

The constitution of the Advisory Council is the subject of sch. 1. There are not less than 20 members, including persons experienced in the practices of medicine, dentistry, veterinary medicine, pharmacy, the pharmaceutical industry and chemistry.

The principle of the 1964, 1965 and 1967 Acts, repealed by s.39 and sch. 6 of the new Act, was that the importing, exporting, production, supply and possession of drugs was lawful, unless the Acts or regulations decreed otherwise. Now the expression "controlled drug" was used to embrace a wide range of drugs which were classified. These even included, for example, sleeping tablets of types which had been the subject of abuse. The controlled drugs were specified in sch. 2 of the Act. It is divided into Part I, in which are listed Class A drugs, such as heroin, Part II, in which are set out Class B drugs, such as cannabis and Part III, in which is contained Class C drugs, such as pemoline. The lists have been compiled largely on the basis of decreasing order of harmfulness, and the penalties vary accordingly. The sch. 2, which can of course be amended by Order in Council, reads:-

PART I

Class A Drugs

1. The following substances and products, namely:-
(a) Acetorphine
    Allylprodine
    Alphacetylmethadol
    Alphameprodine
    Alphamethadol
    Alphaprodine
    Anileridine
    Benzethidine
    Benzylmorphine (3-benzylmorphine)
    Betacetylmethadol
    Betameprodine
    Betamethadol
    Betaprodine
    Bezitramide
    Bufotenine
    Cannabinol, except where contained in cannabis
        or cannabis resin
    Cannabinol derivatives
    Clonitazene
    Coca leaf
    Cocaine

Desomorphine
Dextromoramide
Diamorphine (heroin)
Diampromide
Diethylthiambutene
(Difenoxin added 1975)
Dihydromorphine
Dihydrocodeinone O-carboxymethyloxime
Dimenoxadole
Dimepheptanol
Dimethylthiambutene
Dioxaphetyl butyrate
Diphenoxylate
Dipipanone
(Drotebanol added 1973)
Ecgonine, and any derivatives of ecgonine which is convertible
　　to ecgonine or to cocaine
Ethylmethylthiambutene
Etonitazene
Etorphine
Etoxeridine
Fentanyl
Furethidine
Hydrocodone
Hydromorphinol
Hydromorphone
Hydroxypethidine
Isomethadone
Ketobemidone
Levomethorphan
Levomoramide
Levophenacylmorphan
Levorphanol
Lysergamide
Lysergide and other N-alkyl derivatives of lysergamide
Mescaline
Metazocine
Methadone
Methadyl acetate
Methyldesorphine
Methyldihydromorphine (6-methyldihydromorphine)
Metopon

Morpheridine
Morphine
Morphine methobromide, morphine N-oxide and other
    pentavalent nitrogen morphine derivatives
Myrophine

(Nicodicodine [6-nicotinoyldihydrocodeine] omitted 1973)
Nicomorphine (3, 6-nicotinoylmorphine)
Noracymethadol
Norlevorphanol
Normethadone
Normorphine
Norpipanone
Opium, whether raw, prepared or medicinal
Oxycodone
Oxymorphone
Pethidine
Phenadoxone
Phenampromide
Phenazocine
(Phencyclidine added 1979)
Phenomorphan
Phenoperidine
Piminodine
Piritramide
Poppy-straw and concentrate of poppy-straw
Proheptazine
Properidine (1-methyl-4-phenylpiperidine-4-carboxylic acid
    isopropyl ester)
Psilocin
Racemethorphan
Racemoramide
Racemorphan
Thebacon
Thebaine
Trimeperidine
(4-Bromo-2, 5-dimethoxy-a-methylphenethylamine
    added 1975)
4-Cyano-1-methyl-4-phenyl piperidine
N, N-Diethyltryptamine
N, N-Dimethyltryptamine
2, 5-Dimethoxy-a, 4-dimethyl phenathylamine
1-Methyl-4-phenylpiperidine-4-carboxylic acid

2-Methyl 3-morpholino-1, 1-diphenylpropanecarboxylic acid
4-Phenylpiperidine-4-carboxylic acid ethyl ester

(b) Any compound (not being a compound for the time being specified in sub-paragraph (a) above) structurally derived from tryptamine or from a ring-hydroxy tryptamine by substitution at the nitrogen atom of the sidechain with one or more alkyl substituents but no other substituent.

(c) Any compound (not being methoxyphenamine or a compound for the time being specified in sub-paragraph (a) above) structurally derived from phenethylamine, an N-alkyl-phenethylamine, a-methylphenethylamine, an N-alkyl-a-methylphenethylamine, a-ethylphenethylamine, or an N-alkyl-a-ethylphenethylamine by substitution in the ring to any extent with alkyl, alkoxy, alkylenedioxy or halide substituents, whether or not further substituted in the ring by one or more other univalent substituents.

2. Any *stereoisomeric form* of a *substance* for the time being specified in para. 1 above not being dextromethorphan or dextrorphan.

3. Any ester or ether of a substance for the time being specified in para. 1 or 2 above. (Not being a substance for the time being specified in Part II of this Schedule — added 1973).

4. Any *salt* of a *substance* for the time being specified in any of paras. 1 to 3 above.

5. Any preparation or other product containing a substance or product for the time being specified in any of paras. 1 to 4 above.

6. Any preparation designed for administration by injection which includes a substance or product for the time being specified in any of paras. 1 to 3 of Part II of this Schedule.

PART II

Class B Drugs

1. The following substances and products, namely:-

Acetyldihydrocodeine
Amphetamine
Cannabis and cannabis resin
Codeine
Dexamphetamine
Dihydrocodeine
Ethylmorphine (3-ethylmorphine)
Methylamphetamine
Methylphenidate
Nicocodine
(Nicodicodine added 1973)
Norcodeine
Phenmetrazine
Pholcodine
(Propiram added 1973)

2. Any stereoisomeric form of a substance for the time being specified in para. 1 of this Part of the Schedule.

3. Any salt of a substance for the time being specified in paras 1 or 2 of this Part of the Schedule.

4. Any preparation or other product containing a substance or product for the time being specified in any of paras. 1 to 3 of this Part of the Schedule, not being a preparation falling within para. 6 of Part I of this Schedule.

PART III

Class C Drugs

1. The following substances, namely:-
Benzphetamine
Chlorphentermine
(Fencamfamin omitted 1973)
Mephentermine
Methaqualone
(Pemoline omitted 1973)
Phendimetrazine
(Phentermine omitted 1973)
Pipradrol
(Prolintane omitted 1973)

2.   Any stereoisomeric form of a substance for the time being specified in para. 1 of this Part of this Schedule.

3.   Any salt of a substance for the time being specified in para. 1 or 2 of this Part of this Schedule.

4.   Any preparation or other product containing a substance for the time being specified in any of paras. 1 to 3 of this Part of this Schedule."

Between 1973 and 1975, the 2nd Schedule, as quoted above verbatim from the Act, was changed by the removal from all control of fencamfamin, pemoline, phentermine and prolintane. In 1979, phencyclidine was added.

The principle of the new Act is the opposite of the old, *i.e.* the new principle is first to forbid, and then to create reasonable exceptions for doctors, dentists, veterinary surgeons, pharmacists, hospitals, midwives, ship masters, researchers, *etc.*

Section 2 having defined the expression "controlled drug", ss. 3, 4, 5 and 6 set out the restrictions which are now summarised.

By s.3, the importation and exportation of controlled drugs is prohibited. By s.4, the production, the supply of and the offer to supply controlled drugs is prohibited. By s.5, it is made unlawful to have a controlled drug in one's possession. By s.6, it is unlawful to cultivate any plant of the genus cannabis.

But there are qualifications, and these differ from section to section.

As to s.3 (importation *etc.*) this is permitted under licence from the Home Department and if you can bring yourself under the exceptions contained in regulations made under s.7. These are set out in the Misuse of Drugs Regulations 1973, dealt with hereafter in their proper place. They are amended by S.I. 1974 No. 42, and by S.I. 1975 No. 499.

As to s.4 (production and supply *etc.*) the "regulations" defence applies, and a new defence is introduced by s.28. It is a defence for the accused to prove that he neither knew nor suspected, nor had reason to suspect, the existence of a fact alleged by the prosecution which it is necessary for the prosecution to prove if he is to be convicted of the offence charged. Belief that the drug in question was a controlled drug of a different sort will not, however, afford a defence, unless it can be shown that no offence would have been committed if the facts had been as they were believed to be. In other words, note was taken of the drafting error which led to

Warner's case and *Sweet's* case, noted ante, and presumably the credibility of the accused person will be the major issue when he or she sets up s.28. (See *Ashton-Rickhardt's* case, noted below, in which *Warner's* case was followed).

As to s.5 (possession), the "regulations" defence again applies, as does the s.28 defence. It is also a defence here to prove that, knowing or suspecting the drug to be a controlled drug, the accused took possession of it to prevent another person committing an offence, and destroyed the drug or delivered it to a person lawfully entitled to custody of it. Or, knowing or suspecting it to be a controlled drug, the defendant took possession of it to deliver it into the custody of a person lawfully entitled to custody, and took all reasonable steps to do so. The latter defences apply, with modifications, to charges under s.19 dealing with attempts to commit offences or to incite others to commit offences.

As to s.6 (cannabis cultivation), the s.28 defence applies.

Section 7 is the first "regulation making" section. In addition to exempting such controlled drugs as are specified in the regulations, the regulations make it lawful to commit otherwise forbidden acts under ss. 4, 5 and 6. The regulations may authorise the doing of any thing under a Home Department licence. An order under subs.(4) may be made, in the case of any controlled drug, limiting its production, supply and possession to research or other special purposes. Or such a designation order may make it unlawful for practitioners and pharmacists to supply or possess the designated drug. Such a designation order requires prior consultation with or the recommendation of the Advisory Council. (As to statutory instruments generally see the Statutory Instruments Act 1946).

The next two sections, namely ss. 8 and 9, set out miscellaneous offences involving controlled drugs, *etc.* Miss Stephanie Sweet and the "beatniks" were not overlooked. The addition of the word "knowingly" (an essential ingredient of the offence which has got to be proved) in s.8 was presumably intended to dispel all doubt, and to make assurance doubly sure. Lord Morris had said in *Warner's* case, noted ante: "The presence or absence of the word "knowingly" may in some cases be of great importance in construing particular words in a particular enactment." It may have dawned on the draftsman that the suggestion from Lord Morris was tantamount to an order. Section 8 provides that a person commits an offence if, being the occupier or (note the retention of the words which got Miss Sweet into trouble) concerned in the management of any premises he knowingly permits (see here *Gray's Haulage Co.*

Ltd. v. Arnold [1966] 1 All E.R. 986) or suffers any of the following activities to take place on those premises, that is to say (a) producing or attempting to produce a controlled drug in contravention of s.4(1) of the Act, (b) supplying or attempting to supply a controlled drug to another in contravention of s.4(1) of the Act, or offering to supply a controlled drug to another in contravention of s.4(1), (c) preparing opium for smoking, and (d) smoking cannabis, cannabis resin or prepared opium (defined at s.37(1)). Section 9 enacts that, subject to s.28 before mentioned, it is an offence for a person (a) to smoke or otherwise use prepared opium, or (b) to frequent a place used for the purpose of opium smoking, or (c) to have in his possession any pipes for use in connection with the smoking of opium, or any utensils used in connection with the preparation of opium for smoking. (The words "permits activities to take place" in s.8, instead of "permits premises to be used", are a legacy from the Sweet case).

Sections 10 to 17 set out the powers of the Home Department to prevent the misuse of controlled drugs.

Under s.10, the Secretary of State has power to make such regulations as are needed to prevent such misuse. The regulations may provide that:

(i) precautions must be taken for the safe custody of controlled drugs;

(ii) transactions involving controlled drugs must be the subject of documentation;

(iii) records must be kept and information furnished with respect to controlled drugs;

(iv) precautions taken or records kept may be inspected in pursuance of regulations;

(v) controlled drugs must be properly packed and also labelled;

(vi) the transport of controlled drugs is regulated, and they are destroyed or disposed of when no longer required;

(vii) in regard to prescriptions, the issue of these is regulated, and the supply of controlled drugs on prescriptions is also regulated;

(viii) doctors attending addicts, or suspected addicts, must furnish to the prescribed authority particulars; (see also SI 1973/799)

(ix) the administration and supply by doctors to, and their prescriptions for, addicts and suspected addicts are prohibited except under licence from the Home Department. (See also SI 1973/799).

Section 11 contains power for the Home Department to direct, by notice in writing served on the occupier of any premises on which controlled drugs are kept or to be kept, that special precautions for the safe custody of any controlled drug of a description specified in the notice be taken at the premises. (See also SI 1973/798).

Section 12 enables the Home Department to prohibit practitioners *etc.* convicted of certain offences, namely offences under the 1971 Act and the Customs legislation prohibiting or restricting the importation and exportation of controlled drugs, from, in the case of practitioners, having in possession, prescribing, administering, manufacturing, compounding and supplying, and authorising the administration and supply, of controlled drugs, and in the case of pharmacists, having in possession, manufacturing, compounding and supplying, and supervising and controlling the manufacture, compounding and supply of controlled drugs. Directions under this section prohibiting the prescribing and supply *etc.* of drugs may be cancelled or suspended. It is an offence for a practitioner or pharmacist to contravene such a direction.

Section 13 deals with contraventions by doctors of the regulations, and the terms of their licences, and failure to furnish particulars of drug addicts. The first step is a direction under s. 13 prohibiting the doctor from prescribing, administering *etc.* the controlled drug specified in the direction. Contravention of such a direction constitutes an offence. If a practitioner prescribes, administers *etc.* a controlled drug in an irresponsible manner, a similar direction may be issued. Again, contravention of the direction is an offence. If there are grounds for giving directions under s. 13, the Home Department may, under s. 14, refer the case to a tribunal, constituted in accordance with the Act, for investigation. (See also SI 1974/85(L1)). If the tribunal finds there has been no contravention, and no irresponsible prescribing, and not enough to justify a direction, then no further proceedings ensue. If there is found to have been a contravention, or irresponsibility, then the tribunal may recommend a direction be given indicating the controlled drugs to be specified therein. Notice of the recommendation is served on the offending practitioner, who is invited to submit representations. Representations may be referred to the Advisory Council. On receipt of its advice, the Home Department either gives a direction under s. 13, or refers the case back to the tribunal, or orders that no further proceedings be taken. The procedure is cumbersome, and the power delegated to the tribunal scarcely seems effective. If the circumstances require a direction to be given with a minimum of delay, s. 15 may be invoked. If it is, the case must be referred to a professional panel constituted in accordance with the Act. The practitioner has a right of representation by counsel or solicitor. The period of operation of a direction under s. 13, given by virtue of s. 15, is six weeks.

Section 16 states that sch. 3 of the Act has effect with respect to the constitution and procedure of the tribunal, advisory body and professional panel. The tribunal has five members. The chairman is a barrister, advocate or solicitor. The other four are drawn from professional bodies, depending on whether the respondent is a doctor, dentist or veterinary practitioner or surgeon. Proceedings are held in private, unless the respondent otherwise requests. An advisory body has three members, the chairman being a Q.C. The other two are members of the respondent's profession. A professional panel consists of a chairman and two persons from the respondent's profession.

Section 17 enacts that if, in any area, there is a social problem caused by extensive misuse of dangerous or harmful drugs, the Home Department may, by notice served on any doctor or pharmacist in the area, or on a person carrying on a retail pharmacy business at premises in or in the vicinity of the area, require him to furnish particulars with respect to the number and frequency of occasions on which drugs are prescribed, administered or supplied. It is an offence not to comply with such a requirement. It is an offence, in purported compliance, to give false information. (See *R. v. Kylsant* [1932] 1 K.B. 442).

The next four sections deal with offences. By s. 18, of special concern to practitioners and pharmacists, it is made an offence to contravene regulations. Attempts to commit offences are the subject of s. 19. Section 20 (assisting in or inducing the commission outside the U.K. of an offence punishable under a "corresponding law") — the expression is defined in s. 36(1) — is the same as in the repealed legislation. The procedure to prove the corresponding law is as before — a certificate issued by or on behalf of the foreign State concerned. Section 21 deals with offences by corporations.

Section 22 confers on the Home Department further and extensive regulation-making powers, even enabling it to exclude, by regulations, provisions of the Act creating offences, and provisions of the Customs and Excise Act 1952, applying to the importation and exportation of controlled drugs.

Sections 23 and 24 were and are controversial.

Section 23(1) enacts that a constable or other person authorised by order shall have power to enter the premises of a producer or supplier of controlled drugs and to demand the production of, and to inspect, any books or documents relating to dealings in drugs and to inspect stocks.

By subs. (2), if a constable has reasonable grounds to suspect that any person is in possession of a controlled drug, in contravention of the Act or any regulations, the constable may (a) search that person and detain him for the purpose of searching him, and (b) search any vehicle or vessel in which the constable suspects that the drug may be found, and for that purpose require the person in control of the vehicle or vessel to stop it, and (c) seize and detain, for the purpose of proceedings under the Act, anything found in the course of the search which appears to the constable evidence of an offence under the Act.

By subs. (3), if a justice is satisfied by information that there is reasonable ground for suspecting (a) that any controlled drugs are, in contravention of the Act or regulations, in the possession of a person on any premises, or (4) that a document relating to a transaction which was, or an intended transaction which would if carried out be, an offence, he may grant a search warrant. Such a warrant authorises any constable acting for the area where the premises are to enter the premises, by force if necessary, and to search the premises and any persons therein. If there is reasonable ground for suspecting an offence has been committed in relation to any controlled drugs found on the premises, or in the possession of any person, or such documents as are last mentioned are found, the drugs and documents may be seized and detained.

The final subs. (4) makes it an offence intentionally to obstruct a person in the exercise of powers conferred by s.23, or to conceal drugs *etc.* or without reasonable excuse (proof of which is on the person charged) to fail to produce books or documents when their production is demanded.

By s.24, a constable may arrest without warrant (as to bail, see the Magistrates Courts Act 1952) a person who has committed, or whom the constable with reasonable cause suspects to have committed, an offence under the Act, if (a) he, with reasonable cause, believes that person will abscond unless arrested, or (b) the name and address of that person are unknown to, and cannot be ascertained by him, or (c) he is not satisfied that a name and address furnished by that person as his name and address are true. This section does not prejudice any power of arrest conferred by law apart from the section. (When the search is over, the power to detain lapses, unless the search provides reasonable grounds for arrest.)

Section 25 is concerned with the prosecution and punishment of offences. Schedule 4 informs us of the punishments. After first specifying the section creating the offence, and the general nature of it, it grades the maximum punishment according to whether mode of prosecution is summary or on indictment, and whether a Class A, a Class B, or a Class C drug is involved. It will suffice to give an example. Perhaps the commonest offence is having possession of a controlled drug. The penalty on summary conviction is 12 months or £400 or both (Class A drug), 6 months or £400 or both (Class B drug), and 6 months or £200 or both (Class C drug). On indictment, it is 7 years or a fine or both (Class A drug), 5 years or a fine or both (Class B drug), and 2 years or a fine or both (Class C drug). At the other end of the scale for merely failing to comply with a notice requiring information relating to prescribing, supply *etc.* of drugs, the offender may be let off with a £100 fine. A magistrates' court may try an information for an offence, if the information is laid at any time within 12 months from the commission of the offence.

Section 26 increases the penalties for customs offences, and s.27 deals with forfeiture. The court entering the conviction may order anything shown to relate to the offence to be forfeited and destroyed, or dealt with in such manner as the court orders. Any person claiming to be the owner must have an opportunity to show cause why the order should not be made.

Section 28 has been mentioned. It provides a defence to some offences (offences in regard to production, supply and possession included) if proof is adduced that the accused neither knew nor suspected nor had reason to suspect, the existence of a fact alleged by the prosecution which they have to prove if he is to be convicted. Belief that the drug was a controlled drug of a different sort will not be a defence, unless no offence would have been committed had the facts been as they were believed to be. Sweet's case is thus enacted, but the burden of proof is on the defendant.

Section 29 deals with service of documents. A notice required or authorised by any provision of the Act to be served on any person, may be served on him either by delivering it to him, or leaving it at his proper address, or by sending it by post. In the case of a body corporate, it is duly served on the secretary or clerk. In the case of certain specified notices and directions, if they are served by registered post or recorded delivery, service is deemed to have been effected at the time when the letter containing it would be delivered in the ordinary course of post.

Section 30 enacts that a licence or authority issued by the Home Department may be general or specific, and may be issued on such terms as the Home Department think proper and may be modified or revoked at any time.

By s.31, regulations made by the Home Department may make different provision in relation to different controlled drugs, different classes or persons, different provisions of the Act, or other different cases. They may make the opinion, consent or approval of a prescribed authority or of any person authorised in a prescribed manner material for purposes of any provision of the regulations. Further, these may contain such supplementary provisions as appear expedient to the Home Department. The powers of the Home Department to make regulations under the Act is exercisable by statutory instruments, subject to annulment by resolution of either House. The Home Department must before making regulations consult with the Advisory Council.

By s.32, the Home Department may conduct, or assist in conducting research into any matter relating to the misuse of dangerous or otherwise harmful drugs.

By s.33, the Extradition Act 1870, has effect as if conspiring to commit any offence against any enactment for the time being in force relating to dangerous drugs were included in the list of crimes in sch. 1 to that Act.

Section 34, amending the matrimonial law, to s.40, being the title and commencement, may be skated over, except for s.37, which is the interpretation section. Words and terms are here defined, and among them are:-

(1) Cannabis, meaning (except in the expression "cannabis resin") the flowering or fruiting tops of any plant of the genus cannabis, from which the resin has not been extracted, by whatever name they may be designated and also cannabis resin, meaning the separated resin, whether crude or purified, obtained from any plant of the genus cannabis — a definition slightly amended by the Criminal Law Act 1977, s.52, so as to outlaw cannabis leaves as well. Section 52 is hereafter set out in its proper place.

(2) Produce, meaning producing a controlled drug by manufacture, cultivation or any other method.

(3) Supply, meaning not only supplying but distributing as well.

It is further provided by subs. (2) that references in the Act to misusing a drug are references to misusing it by taking it, and taking it means any form of self-administration whether or not involving assistance by another. For the purpose of the Act, the things which a person had in his possession include any thing subject to his control which is in the custody of another.

The Act extends to Northern Ireland (s.40).

VI

The effect of the Misuse of Drugs Act 1971 on five other enactments may next be shortly mentioned. These are ss. 45, 56 and 304 of the Customs and Excise Act 1952, the Extradition Act 1932, s.1, the Extradition Act 1870, sch. 1, and the Matrimonial Proceedings (Magistrates' Courts) Act 1960, s.16, and the Criminal Law Act 1967, s.2.

Section 45 of the 1952 Act provides that if any person unships or lands in any port or unloads from any aircraft in the United Kingdom or from any vehicle in Northern Ireland or removes from their places of importation or from any approved wharf, examination station, transit shed or customs station, any goods imported, landed or unloaded, contrary to any prohibition or restriction for the time being in force under or by virtue of any enactment with respect of those goods, or assists or is otherwise concerned in such unshipping, landing, unloading or removal, or if any person imports or is concerned in importing any goods contrary to any such prohibition or restriction as aforesaid, he is liable to a penalty. If he imports or causes to be imported any goods concealed in a container holding goods of a different description, he is liable to a large penalty.

By s.56, if any goods are exported or brought to any place in the U.K. for the purpose of being exported, and the exportation is or would be contrary to any prohibition or restriction for the time being in force with respect to those goods under or by virtue of any enactment, the goods shall be liable to forfeiture, and the exporter or intending exporter of the goods, and any agent of his concerned in the exportation or intended exportation, shall be liable to a penalty. Any person knowingly concerned in the exportation or attempted exportation shall also be liable to a penalty.

By s.304, if any person knowingly, with intent to evade any prohibition or restriction for the time being in force under or by virtue of any enactment with respect thereto, acquires possession of, or is in any way concerned in carrying, removing, depositing, harbouring, keeping or concealing or in any manner dealing with any goods with respect to the importation or exportation of which any prohibition or restriction is for the time being in force, or is knowingly concerned in any fraudulent evasion or attempt at evasion, of any such prohibition or restriction as aforesaid, he may be detained and is liable to a penalty.

Practitioners and pharmacists convicted of offences under these sections are dealt with under s.12 of the 1971 Act. the Home Department may give a direction under subs. (2) prohibiting them in future from possessing, prescribing, administering, *etc.* controlled drugs.

Further, by s.26 of the 1971 Act, the penalties are increased. If the drug imported or exported is a Class A or Class B drug, on summary conviction the penalty is three times the value of the goods or £400, and/or 12 months. On indictment, the fine has no limit, and term of imprisonment is up to 14 years.

Section 19 of the Extradition Act 1870, provided that where, in pursuance of any arrangement with a foreign state, any person accused or convicted of any crime which, if committed in England, would be one of the crimes described in the first Schedule, is surrendered by that foreign state, such person shall not, until he had been restored or had an opportunity of returning to such foreign state, be triable or tried for any offence committed prior to the surrender in any part of H.M. dominions other than such of the said crimes as may be proved by the facts on which the surrender is grounded. Dangerous drugs being then lawful, s.1 of the Extradition Act 1932, enacted that the 1870 Act be construed as if offences against any enactment for the time being in force relating to dangerous drugs, and attempts to commit such offences, were included in the list of crimes in the first Schedule. Now, by s.33 of the 1971 Act, conspiring to commit any offence against any enactment for the time being in force relating to dangerous drugs is included in the list of crimes in sch. 1 to the 1870 Act.

Under s.1 of the Matrimonial Proceedings Act 1960, if your spouse is a drug addict, that is a cause of complaint, which may lead to an order under the Act. "Drug Addict" is now defined (by s.16(1)) as a person (not being a mentally disordered person) who, by reason of the habitual taking or using, otherwise than upon medical advice, of any controlled drug within the meaning of the Misuse of Drugs Act 1971, is at times dangerous to himself or to others, or is incapable of managing himself or his affairs, or so conducts himself that it would not be reasonable to expect a spouse of ordinary sensibilities to continue to cohabit with him.

There is apparently no decision of the courts as to the meaning of the term "ordinary sensibilities". It may well be that it is differently interpreted in different districts. Apparently it is not necessary for a complainant to prove the absence of medical authority to take drugs. Orders on this ground are rarely made. Usually, constructive desertion is pleaded.

The powers given to a constable under s.2 of the Criminal Law Act 1967, to arrest anyone whom he, with reasonable cause, suspects to have committed an offence, and to enter and search any place where that person is or is suspected to be, are not touched by the later Acts.

VII

It is felt that a case chapter may be of assistance to those facing problems in this complex field of law. The number of cases is not small, and only a selection can be made. The reader may feel he would have chosen differently, but a choice has had to be made.

A.   Section 4 — Supplying, producing *etc.* a controlled drug.

Haggard and Mason, [1976] 120 S.J. 7. The defendant bought a piece of blotting paper impregnated with what he believed to be LSD. He intended to resell the substance for profit and offered some of it to a prospective buyer. The sale went through. Both parties were unaware that it was Bromo STP, a drug not controlled. The defendant was convicted of offering to supply a controlled drug. The justices convicted, and made an order under s.27 that the remaining drops of Bromo STP be forfeited and that £146, the remainder of the illegal proceeds be forfeited. Held, the justices were right to convict. The offence was completed at the time the defendant offered to sell LSD. But there was no power to order the forfeiture of the £146.

R. v. Nock; R. v. Alsford [1978] 122 S.J. 417. The defendants agreed together to produce cocaine by separating it from the other substances in a powder which they believed to be a mixture of cocaine and liquocaine hydrochloride but contained no cocaine, so that cocaine could not have been produced from it. They were convicted of conspiracy to produce a controlled drug, cocaine, in contravention of s.4. Held by the House of Lords, the conviction was wrong. To agree to pursue a course of conduct which, if carried out in accordance with the intention of those agreeing to it, would not amount to or involve the commission of any offence, did not amount to a criminal conspiracy at common law, or under the Criminal Law Act 1977. The agreement between the defendants was to pursue a course of action which could never have produced cocaine.

R. v. Harris [1979] Law Guardian 321. The defendant and others attempted to make amphetamine. They had the right formula, but obtained formaldehyde instead of formamide. When they mixed the chemicals in a pan on a stove, they only produced smoke and smell. They failed to produce amphetamine — one ingredient was wrong and they lacked the knowledge. Held by the Court of Appeal, there was an agreement to do an unlawful act which was inherently possible. It was not within the boundaries of *R. v. Nock* (supra), because the purpose there embarked upon, the production of cocaine from liquacaine hydrochloride, would have required not a chemist but an alchemist.

B.   Section 5 — Possession of drug.

Bocking v. Robers [1973] 117 s.J. 581. A hookah pipe belonging to the defendant was found, by chemical analysis, to contain traces of cannabis resin. The quantity was too small to be weighed, but was more than 20 micrograms, because below that amount the method of analysis used would not give a positive indication. He was charged with being in possession of cannabis. Held, the court should use common sense and not a mathematical formula. The quantity was measurable, being at least 20 micrograms. The conviction was correct. The decision in *Bocking v. Roberts* was considered, but not over ruled, in the later case *R. v. Carver [1978] T. L. Reports* (noted infra).

R. v. Wright [1975] 119 S.J. 825. The defendant, a passenger in a car, threw out of one of its windows a tin, later found to contain cannabis resin, on being told by the driver to throw it away. He was convicted of possessing a controlled drug. His defence was that he had no cannabis himself, and was not aware that anyone in the car had any, but the driver had handed him something, and told him to throw it out of the window. His conviction was quashed. It was held by the Court of Appeal, that if a person was handed a container, and at the moment when he received it did not know or suspect or have reason to suspect that it contained drugs, and if, before he had time to examine the contents, he was told to throw it away, and he did so immediately, he could not be said to have been in possession of the drugs which happened to be inside the container so as to be guilty of an offence under s.5. *Warner*'s case (noted ante) was applied. The trial judge had wrongly directed the jury. He gave them no help about the mental element necessary for the proof of the offence.

Holmes v. Chief Constable of Merseyside [1976], *The Times,* December 24, 1975. The defendant was charged with possessing a controlled drug with intent to supply it to another contrary to s.5. He submitted he had been holding drugs on behalf of himself and others, that the group was in joint possession of them and that a division of drugs was not "supplying". He was convicted, the trial judge ruling that the defence was invalid in law. The Appeal Court agreed with the ruling, but the appeal was allowed on other grounds, and a rehearing ordered before another judge. By s.37 of the Act, "supplying" included distributing. The word "supply" must be given its ordinary meaning. A person who went shopping for drugs for himself and others was "supplying" the drugs, because distribution was a form of supply. The existence of a co-operation enterprise made no difference.

R. v. Ashton-Rickhardt [1977] 121 s.J. 774. During a search of the defendant's car, police officers found a reefer which, on analysis, contained 200 milligrammes of cannabis. He was charged with possessing a controlled drug contrary to s.5. His defence was that the reefer had been left in his car by an acquaintance, without his knowledge. The judge did not direct the jury that the Crown had to prove that the defendant had knowledge of the presence of the article, and he directed them that the defendant had to disprove knowledge. The appeal was allowed. Putting the question of the proof of want of knowledge of the presence of the article directly on the defence was wrong and contrary to *Warner*'s case (noted ante). The House of Lords, in *Warner*'s case, had laid down that there could not be possession of a controlled drug, unless the accused knew the "thing" alleged contained the drug in his possession. Knowledge was an essential prerequisite to proof by the prosecution of possession. The argument for the Crown, that s.28 of the 1971 Act put the whole burden of disproving knowledge on the defendant, was wrong. The purpose of s.28 was to afford a defence where none had previously existed, and there was nothing in s.28 which altered the burden which rested on the Crown. The word "possession" in s.5 had the same meaning as it was given in *Warner*'s case. Section 28 did not affect it in any way. Mr. Ashton-Rickardt's appeal was allowed. (See Smith and Hogan's "Criminal Law" for a fuller discussion of *Warner, Ashton-Rickardt* and other cases.)

Jeffrey v. Black [1977] 121 S.J. 662. The defendant was arrested for stealing a sandwich from a public house. He was taken to the police station. The police said they intended to search his premises. He did not reply but accompanied them to his house. The police searched and found cannabis. The defendant appeared before the justices, charged with both the theft and also the possession of cannabis. When the police were about to give evidence of what they found, the defendant objected on the ground that since there had been no consent to the police entering the room, the evidence of what they found was inadmissible. The prosecutor's appeal was allowed. The Divisional Court held, that if the police had considered that, as a result of the theft of the sandwich, it was necessary to search the premises, they could have done so without further authority. When the officers entered the room, they were not concerned with the sandwich, but with the completely different matter of whether they would find drugs. The common law had not yet arrived at the point where police officers, who arrested a person at one place, could then search his house at another place, when there was no connection between the house contents and the offence charged, nor was there evidence from the house to support the offence. Nevertheless, although the entry was unlawful, that did not prevent the evidence found being relevant and admissible. An irregularity in obtaining evidence did not render it inadmissible. The justices had discretion to decline to admit prosecution evidence, if it would be unfair or oppressive to admit it. The discretion should only be exercised in exceptional circumstances, when the police had not only acted without authority, but also in some other way which was reprehensible, for example they had been guilty of trickery, or had misled someone, or had been unfair or oppressive.

R. v. Klug [1977] *The Times*, November 23, 1977. The defendant, a West German, was found to be in possession of cannabis oil at London Airport, when in transit from India to Berlin. He was convicted, and his appeal was dismissed. The Court of Appeal decided that the English courts could not say that, as long as the offender went away, he did not need punishment.

R. v. Goodchild [1977] 1WLR 473, and *R. v. Goodchild (No. 2)* [1978] 122 S.J. 263. The defendant was travelling by car. The police searched it. They found cigarettes and a green leaf substance. The cigarettes contained cannabis plant material. Later, at Goodchild's house, a green leaf substance was found, and this on analysis contained cannabis plant material. After much litigation, it was held that he was not in possession of cannabis — the leaves were not part of the "flowering or fruiting tops" (see s.37 of the 1971 Act, as originally framed). He was not guilty of possessing a cannabinol derivative either. The possession of naturally occurring leaf and stalk of cannabis, of which a cannabinol derivative (THC, see Chapter 1) was an *unseparated* constituent, could not be charged under the 1971 Act as possession of a cannabinol derivative. While s.52 of the 1977 Act (noted ante) now states that "cannabis" (except in the expression "cannabis resin") means any plant of the genus cannabis or any part of any such plant (by whatever name designated) except that it does not include cannabis resin or any of the following products after separation from the rest of the plant, namely, the mature stalk of any such plant, and fibre produced from mature stalk of any such plant, and seed of any plant, the *Goodchild* cases have left something behind. Only the definition of cannabis has been changed. People have been dealt with on charges of being in possession of mushrooms containing the hallucinogenic drug psilocybin. Prosecutions pending in 1977 and 1978 have been dropped, because it is not an offence to possess a drug contained inside a plant. Other plants contain controlled drugs, morning glory being an example.

R. v. Carver [1978], *The Times*, May 10, 1978. The defendant possessed a roach end (a filter made of rolled cardboard) which contained some 20 microgrammes (invisible to the naked eye) of cannabis resin, and a wooden box, scraping from which produced two milligrammes of cannabis resin, two pinheads in size. He was charged with unlawful possession of cannabis resin. The amount of the drug on which his conviction was based was so small, that there was no way at all in which cannabis in that quantity could have been used in any manner which it was intended by the misuse of drugs legislation to prohibit. The Court of Appeal quashed the conviction. If the quantity of the drug found in a case like this is so minute as to amount to nothing, or if the quantity is so minute that it is unusable in any manner which the 1971 Act is intended to prohibit, a conviction for being in possession of the minute quantity of the drug is not justified.

Muir v. Smith [1978], *The Times*, February 17, 1978. Muir was charged with being in possession of cannabis resin. The Crown Court was satisfied he was in possession of a prohibited substance, in the form of cannabis resin or herbal cannabis. They were not satisfied that the prohibited substance was cannabis resin. Held, by the Divisional Court, that if the prosecutor could not distinguish between cannabis resin and herbal cannabis, the conviction should be quashed. Nobody knew whether the substance was cannabis resin or herbal cannabis. Until that problem could be solved, there could be no conviction for possession of cannabis resin.

R. v. Malcolm [1978], *The Times*, May 6, 1978. The defendant was charged with possessing 0.584 grammes of cannabis, and supplying cannabis. The material in his possession was the flowering or fruiting tops of the cannabis plant. There was resin in the material. It could not be extracted without a great deal of trouble. Held, if resin was in the very part of the plant possessed, it made no difference that it was difficult to extract. The parts in Malcolm's possession were within the definition that cannabis (except in the expression cannabis resin), meant the flowering or fruiting tops of the plant.

R. v. Lidiard [1978] 122 S.J. 743. The defendant was seen by police officers to throw a pipe over a wall. He denied the pipe was his. He admitted he knew it had been used for smoking cannabis. He was tried on the day before Carver's case. He was advised, on the authority of *Bocking v. Roberts* (noted ante) to plead guilty. He did so, and appealed against conviction. The Court of Appeal declined to comment on the merits of his defence (his comments to the police showed he might have a valid excuse, if the police put their case on a broader basis than possession of a tiny amount of cannabis, and the prosecution accepted that it was a defence of sorts), but decided the verdict was unsatisfactory, and allowed the appeal. The enlarged jurisdiction of the court under s.44 of the Criminal Law Act 1977, was relevant.

Kwan Ping Bong v. The Queen [1979] 2 W.L.R. 433. This was an appeal from Hong Kong to the Judicial Committee of the Privy Council. It is of interest only for the following extract, from the judgment of Lord Diplock (p. 438): "Where, as is not uncommon in modern legislation dealing with drugs, there is provision that, on proof by the prosecution of the existence of certain facts, some other fact shall be presumed to exist unless the contrary is proved, the effect of the provision is to convert an inference which at common law the jury would not be entitled to draw, unless they were satisfied beyond all reasonable doubt that it was right, into an inference which they are bound to draw, unless they are satisfied that on the balance of probabilities it is wrong."

C.   Section 8 — Permitting premises to be used.

R. v. Tao [1976] 120 S.J. 420. A student lived in a university college hostel. The college authorities had power to enter his room at any time. In the student's absence, police discovered cannabis in his room. A man was standing nearby, who was later convicted of possessing cannabis. The student was convicted under s.8, in that, being the occupier of premises, he permitted them to be used for smoking cannabis. Held, a person who had a contractual licence to be in exclusive occupation of premises, with the power to exclude those who might use the premises for forbidden purposes, was an occupier for the purposes of the Act. The student had a contractual licence from the college authorities so to occupy the premises, and was rightly convicted.

R. v. Josephs and Christie. The Times, February 26, 1977. The defendants were charged with being concerned in the management of premises on which they knowingly permitted the supply of a controlled drug contrary to s.8. They ran a card school, in the basement of a house owned, but not occupied by the local council. They were in a sense squatters. The police found cannabis. Packets of cannabis were in the possession of a man, who had been with the two defendants. The defendants argued that they could not be concerned with the management, unless there was some sort of authority, giving them a legal right. Held, if in truth a man was exercising control over premises, running them or organising or managing them, the fact that he was not legally in possession of them was irrelevant. The conviction was upheld.

D.   Section 304 — Smuggling, importation, *etc.*

R. v. Arcadan [1972] 116 S.J. 237. The defendants were charged with conspiracy to commit an offence against s.304 of the Customs and Excise Act 1952, a conspiracy to acquire possession of cannabis. Two packing cases containing cannabis were sent from Beirut to London Airport. Several days later, they were redelivered to a London hotel, at the direction of one of the defendants. The defendants were arrested. At the trial, it was submitted on their behalf that the chairman should withdraw the case from the jury, on the grounds that nothing had happened which was capable of amounting to the conspiracy charged, in that, whatever was done at a place so physically remote from the airport, and so long after the importation, there could be no offence against s.304. The conviction was upheld. The Court of Appeal said no distinction could be drawn between goods imported with intent to evade duty (when a person was guilty if the acts were done a long time after and at a place far from their importation), and goods the importation of which was prohibited by statute. The appeal was dismissed.

R. v. Wall [1974]. *The Times*, March 6, 1974. The defendant was convicted of being knowingly concerned in the fraudulent evasion of the restriction imposed by statute on the importation of cannabis, on February 17, 1973, contrary to s.304. Evidence was given that on that date Wall's co-defendants brought a van from Calais to Folkestone. It contained cannabis. Wall told the police he had left the U.K. in December 1972. He agreed that he had gone in the van with a co-defendant. He said he had been to Afghanistan and had flown back to the U.K. in January 1973. He appealed against his conviction. He claimed that he had done nothing relevant on February 17, 1973, and what he had done was not in England. His appeal was dismissed. The Appeal Court said that acts done abroad to further the evasion of a restriction on importation of drugs into the U.K. were punishable. If it were not so a person abroad who slipped a package containing a drug into the luggage of an innocent passenger, who then brought it into the U.K., would be exempt from punishment.

R. v. Vickers [1975] 1W.L.R. 811. Mr. Vickers was charged with conspiring in the U.K. to assist in the commission of an offence, punishable under American law, by conspiring to assist the importation of cannabis or cannabis resin into the United States. In August 1973, in England, he agreed with Morris that he, Vickers, would hire a truck, and collect and load in London cabinets filled with baffles, and transport the same via Dover to Italy, knowing that thereafter cannabis from an unknown source would be fitted into the cabinets, and shipped by Morris and others to the States, in contravention of their drugs legislation (a "corresponding law"). A person commits an offence if, in the U.K., he assists in or induces the commission in any place, outside the U.K., of an offence punishable under the provisions of a corresponding law in force in that place. Mr. Vickers was held guilty — the agreement with Morris was to participate in a course of action, the historical consequence of which was the illegal importation of cannabis into the United States. (See s.20 of the 1971 Act.)

R. v. Green [1976] 2 W.L.R. 57. In August 1873, the customs opened a crate which arrived at Southampton. They found cannabis. They removed it, and substituted peat and paper. In September, the crate was collected and delivered to a garage in London, which had been rented by the defendant, Green, using a false name. Customs officers charged Green with an offence of being concerned in the fraudulent evasion of the prohibition on the importation of cannabis, under s.304, and with conspiring to evade the prohibition. Held, by the Court of Appeal, evasion was established. It was a continuing offence, which did not cease when the cannabis was seized. The renting of the garage, to store the cannabis, completed the offence under s.304. It was no defence that the unlawful purpose of the conspirators could not be achieved.

R. v. Kence [1978], *The Times*, April 15, 1978. Kence, an Australian, agreed when he was in Bangkok on his way to West Germany, to go to Bogota. There he collected cocaine. He stopped at London to see his girl friend. 194 grams of cocaine were found in his stockings. He was charged with being concerned in the evasion of the prohibition on importation of cocaine under s.304, as amended by s.26 of the 1971 Act. He appealed against his sentence of 3 years imprisonment, pleading in vain for some other punishment to be substituted, on the ground that the cocaine was not to be used or sold in the U.K. He was in transit. The court held that such considerations as transit were relevant, but their weight was small. Three years was a reasonable and moderate punishment.

R. v. Menocal [1978] 122 s.J. 661. Mrs. Menocal was a drug smuggler. She imported cocaine contrary to s.304 of the 1952 Act. She was sentenced to imprisonment. More than 3 months later, an order was made under s.27 of the Misuse of Drugs Act 1971, or s.43 of the Powers of Criminal Courts Act 1973, forfeiting money which was in her possession when she was being arrested. Held, an order under s.27 of the 1971 Act had the object of protection of the public, and was not in the nature of a sentence. The forfeiture order under s.27 of the 1971 Act was valid. The woman's appeal against the order was accordingly dismissed by the Court of Appeal.

As this work was going to press, an important judgment of the Court of appeal, *R. v. Chatwood and Others* (1980) 124 SJ 396, was delivered.

The facts were that the defendants were experienced drug takers. They were questioned by the police, and made oral and written admissions that each of them had injected himself with drugs, including heroin. Each defendant pleaded not guilty to contravening s.5(1) of the Misuse of Drugs Act 1971 by unlawful possession of the drugs which he had admitted having used for injecting himself. The prosecution adduced no scientific evidence of analysis. The defendants, at the close of the prosecutor's case, submitted that there was no case to answer in the absence of scientific analysis evidence. Only one defendant gave evidence, stating that the substance with which he had injected himself was flour. The jury convicted the defendants, whose appeals were dismissed. Forbes J. said that, since the defendants were experienced drug takers, their statements to the police were sufficient to provide prima facie evidence of the nature of the substance which had been in their possession. Therefore, there was a case against them for the defendants to answer. In view of the jury's verdict they disbelieved the evidence by the defendant who gave it, that he had used flour, and they believed his admissions to the police.

VIII

The Misuse of Drugs (Notification of and Supply to Addicts) Regulations 1973 came into operation on July 1st, 1973. They replaced the Dangerous Drugs (Notification of Addicts) Regulations 1968, and the Dangerous Drugs (Supply to Addicts) Regulations 1968.

The controlled drugs to which the Regulations apply are:–

1. The following substances and products namely:

   Cocaine
   Methadone
   Dextromoramide
   Morphine
   Diamorphine (heroin)
   Opium
   Dipipanone
   Oxycodone
   Hydrocodone
   Pethidine
   Hydromorphone
   Phenagocine
   Levorphanol
   Piritramide

2. Any stereoisomeric form of a substance specified in paragraph 1 above, not being destrorphan.
3. Any ester or ether of a substance specified in 1 or 2 above not being a substance for the time being specified in Part II of sch. 2 of the Misuse of Drugs Act 1971.
4. Any salt of a substance specified in any of paras. 1 to 3 above.
5. Any preparation or other product containing a substance or product specified in any of paras. 1 to 4 above.

   Any doctor who attends a person he considers or suspects to be addicted to any controlled drug must within seven days furnish in writing to the Home Department such of the following particulars with respect to that person as are known, i.e. the name, address, sex, date of birth and national health service number of that person and the name of the drug.

   It is unnecessary to furnish these details if:
   (a) the doctor is of the opinion that the continued administration of

46

the drug is required for treating organic disease or injury; or
(b) the particulars have during the previous twelve months been furnished by the doctor, or another doctor in the same form, or the doctor's employer or principal, or a hospital doctor, or a nursing home doctor.

A doctor must not administer or supply to a person he considers, or suspects, to be addicted to a drug, or authorise the administration or supply to such a person or prescribe for such a person, any of the following controlled drugs:–
(a) cocaine, its salts and any preparation or other product containing cocaine or its salts other than a preparation falling within para. 2 of sch. 1 to the Misuse of Drugs Regulations 1973.
(b) diamorphine, its salts and any preparation or other product containing diamorphine or its salts.

The exceptions to this last rule are:–
(a) If the administration or supply is for the purpose of treating organic disease or injury;
(b) If the administration or supply is under and in accordance with a Home Department licence in pursuance of the Regulations.
(c) If the administration or supply is authorised by another doctor under and in accordance with a licence issued to him in pursuance of the Regulations.

Licences issued under the revoked 1968 Regulations before July 1st, 1973, continued in force after that date.

A person is defined as being addicted to a drug if, and only if, he has as a result of repeated administration become so dependant on the drug that he has an overpowering desire for the administration of it to be continued.

These Regulations apply to servants and agents of the Crown, and are made under S5, 10, 22 and 30 of the 1971 Act.

IX

The use of controlled drugs in medicine, dentistry, pharmacy, midwifery, etc. is permitted by the Misuse of Drugs Regulations 1973. These make lawful the necessary activities of practitioners, chemists, hospitals, etc. in their daily work. The Schedules to the Misuse of Drugs Act 1971, are of interest to judges, lawyers, magistrates and police officers. They are of no use to pharmacists, or others engaged in the practice of medicine.

But, in the Misuse of Drugs Regulations 1973, the controlled drugs are classified in four Schedules, ascending to different levels of control. The purpose of the Schedules has nothing to do with penalties. That is the concern of the Act.

Schedule 1 contaires preparations of certain controlled drugs, e.g. cocaine, codeine, morphine, combined with other substances in such small amounts or in such ways that they are not liable to produce dependence, or cause harm if they are misused.

Schedule 2 includes major stimulants, e.g. amphetamines, and the opiates, e.g. heroin, methadone, and morphine.

Schedule 3 includes minor stimulants, such As benzphetamine, drugs not as likely to be misused as Sch. 2 drugs.

Schedule 4 includes the hallucinogenic drugs, e.g. L.S.D. and cannabis, with virtually no therapeutic uses.

The four Schedules are now reproduced and read:

SCHEDULE 1

1. (1)Any preparation of one or more of the substances to which this paragraph applies, not being a preparation designed for administration by injection, when compounded with one or more other active or inert ingredients and containing a total of not more than 100 milligrammes of the substance or substances (calculated as base) per dosage unit and with a total concentration of not more than 2.5 per cent. (calculated as base) in undivided preparations.

    (2)The substances to which this paragraph applies are acetyldihydrocodeine, codeine, dihydrocodeine, ethylmorphine, nicocodine, nicodicodine (6-nicotinoyldihydrocodeine), norcodeine, pholcodine and their respective salts.

2. Any preparation of cocaine containing not more than 0.1 per cent. of cocaine calculated as cocaine base, being a preparation

compounded with one or more other active or inert ingredients in such a way that the cocaine cannot be recovered by readily applicable means or in a yield which would constitute a risk to health.

3. Any preparation of medicinal opium or of morphine containing (in either case) not more than 0.2 per cent of morphine calculated as anhydrous morphine base, being a preparation compounded with one or more other active or inert ingredients in such a way than the opium, or, as the case may be, the morphine, cannot be recovered by readily applicable means or in a yield which would constitute a risk to health.

4. Any preparation of diphenoxylate containing, per dosage unit, not more than 2.5 milligrammes of diphenoxylate calculated as base, and a quantity of atropine sulphate equivalent to at least 1 per cent. of the dose of diphenoxylate.

5. Any powder of ipecacuanha and opium comprising-
10 per cent. opium, in powder,
10 per cent. ipecacuanha root, in powder
well mixed with
80 per cent. of any other powdered ingredient containing no controlled drug.

6.

Any mixture containing one or more of the preparations specified in paras. 1 to 5, being a mixture of which none of the other ingredients is a controlled drug.

SCHEDULE 2

1. The following substances and products, namely:−

Acetorphine.
Allylprodine.
Alphacetylmethadol.
Alphameprodine.
Alphamethadol.
Alphaprodine.
Anileridine.
Benzethidine.
Benzylmorphine. (3-benzylmorphine).
Betacetylmethadol.
Betameprodine.
Betamethadol.

Betaprodine.
Bezitramide.
Clonitazene.
Cocaine.
Desomorphine.
Dextromoramide.
Diamorphine.
Diampromide.
Diethylthiambutene.
Dihydrocodeinone O-carboxymethyloxime.
Dihydromorphine.
Dimenoxadole.
Dimepheptanol.
Dimethylthiambutene.
Dioxaphetylbutyrate.
Diphenoxylate.
Dipipanone.
Drotebanol (3,4-dimethoxy-17-methyl-morphinan-6B, 14-diol).
Ecgonine, and any derivative of ecgonine which is convertible to exgonine or to cocaine.
Ethylmethylthiambutene.
Etonitazene.
Etorphine.
Etoxeridine.
Fentanyl.
Furethidine.
Hydrocodone.
Hydromorphinol.
Hydromorphone.
Hydroxypethidine.
Isomethadone.
Ketobemidone.
Levomethorphan.
Levomoramide.
Levophenacylmorphan.
Levorphanol.
Medicinal opium.
Metazocine.
Methadone.
Methadyl acetate.
Methyldesorphine.
Methyldihydromorphine (6-methyldihydromorphine).
Metopon.

Morpheridine.
Morphine.
Morphine Methobromide, morphine N-oxide and other
pentavalent nitrogen morphine derivatives.
Myrophine.
Nicomorphine.
Noracymethadol.
Norlevorphanol.
Normethadone.
Normorphine.
Norpipanone.
Oxycodone.
Oxymorphone.
Pethidine.
Phenadoxone.
Phenampromide.
Phenazocine.
(Phenazclidine added 1979).
Phenomorphan.
Phenoperidine.
Piminodine.
Piritramide.
Proheptazine.
Properidine.
Racemethorphan.
Racemoramide.
Racemorphan.
Thebacon.
Thebaine.
Trimeperidine.
4-Cyano-2-dimethylamino-4, 4 diphenylbutane.
4-Cyano-1-methyl-4-phenylpiperidine.
1-Methyl-4-phenylpiperidine-4-carboxylic acid.
2-Methyl-3-morpholino-1, 1-diphenylpropanecarboxylic acid.
4-Phenylpiperidine-4-carboxylic acid ethyl ester.

2.   Any steroisomeric form of a substance specified in para. 1 not
being dextromethorphan or dextrorphan.
3.   Any ester or ether of a substance specified in para. 1 or 2, not
being a substance specified in para. 6.
4.   Any salt of a substance specified in any of paras. 1 to 3.
5.   Any preparation or other product containing a substance or

51

product specified in any of paras. 1 to 4, not being a preparation specified in sch. 1.

6.   The following substances and products, namely:–

Acetyldihydrocodeine.
Amphetamine.
Codeine.
Dexamphetamine.
Dihydrocodeine.
Ethylmorphine (3-ethylmorphine).
methaqualone.
Methylamphetamine.
Methylphenidate.
Nicocodine.
Nicodicodine (6-nicotinoyldi-hydrocodeine).
Norcodeine.
Phenmetrazine.
Pholcodine.
Propiram.

7.   Any stereoisomeric form of a substance specified in para.6.
8.   Any salt of a substance specified in para. 6 or 7.
9.   Any preparation or other product containing a substance or product specified in any of paras. 6 to 8, not being a preparation specified in sch. 1.

SCHEDULE 3

1.   The following substances, namely:–

Benzphetamine.
Chlorphentermine.
Mephentermine.
Phendimetrazine.
Pipradol.

2.   Any stereoisomeric form of a substance specified in para. 1.
3.   Any salt of a substance specified in para. 1 or 2.
4.   Any preparation or other product containing a substance specified in any of paras. 1 to 3, not being a preparation specified in sch. 1.

SCHEDULE 4

1. The following substances and products, namely:–

Bufotenine.
Cannabinol.
Cannabinol derivatives.
Cannabis and cannabis resin.
Coca leaf.
Concentrate of poppy-straw.
Lysergamide.
2,5-Dimethoxy-a,4-dimethyl-phenethylamine.
Lysergide and other.
N-alkyl derivatives of.
Lysergamide.
Mescaline.
Raw opium.
Psilocin.
N,N-Diethyltrptamine.
N,N-Dimethyltrptamine.

2. Any stereoisomeric form of a substance specified in para. 1.
3. Any ester or ether of a substance specified in para. 1. or 2.
4. Any salt of a substance specified in any of paras. 1 to 3.
5. Any preparation or other product containing a substance or product specified in any of paras. 1 to 4, not being a preparation specified in sch. 1.

The exemptions may be classified as under:

Possession.   By reg. 4 (1), the provisions of the Act prohibiting the possession of controlled drugs do not apply to any of the controlled drugs in sch. 1, and by reg. 5, licence holders may possess drugs in accordance with the terms of their licences.
          By reg. 6, a general authority to possess any controlled drug is conferred on constables acting in the course of their duties; on carriers acting on the course of their business; on Post Office employees acting in the course of their business; on officers of customs and excise acting in the course of their duties; on laboratory workers to whom drugs have been sent for forensic

examination in the course of their duties; and on persons engaged in conveying drugs to persons authorised by the Regulations to possess them.

By reg. 10, (1), Sch. 2 and sch. 3 drugs may be possessed by practitioners, pharmacists, persons conducting retail pharmacy businesses, matrons of hospitals or nursing homes, hospital ward or theatre sisters, laboratory researchers, public analysts, sampling officers, testers of drugs, and pharmaceutical society inspectors. This is an abbreviated list of the persons specified in regs. 8 (2) and 9 (2).

By reg. 10 (2), a person may possess sch. 2 or 3 drugs, for administration for medical, dental or veterinary purposes, in accordance with the directions of a practitioner. But this does not apply if the patient was being supplied by another doctor with a drug, and failed to disclose this. Nor does it apply if a false statement was made to obtain the prescription.

By reg. 10 (4), persons whose names are entered in registers kept for the purposes of the Regulations by the Home Department may possess sch. 3 drugs, in the case of the first specified register, and drugs which they lawfully produce as supply in the case of the other registers.

By reg. 10 (5), ship owners and ship masters, if the ship has no doctor, masters of foreign ships docking at U.K. ports, and installation managers of offshore installations, may possess sch. 2 or 3 drugs.

By ref. 11 (1), certified midwives may possess pethidine, provided they have obtained it on a midwife's supply order signed by the "appropriate medical officer" - the doctor authorised by the local supervising authority for the region or area. Importation And Exportation. By reg. 4 (1), controlled drugs in sch. 1 may be freely imported and exported.

Administration. By reg. 7 (1), any person may administer to another a sch. 1 drug.

By reg. 7 (2), a doctor or dentist may administer sch. 2 or 3 drugs to patients.

By reg. 7 (3), any person may administer to a patient, in accordance with a doctor's or a dentist's directions, a sch. 2 or 3 drug.

By reg. 11 (1) (b), a certified midwife may adminster pethidine.

Manufacturing and Compounding. By reg. 8 (1) and 9 (1), practitioners and pharmacists may manufacture or compound sch. 1

or 2 drugs, and also sch. 3 drugs. So may persons lawfully conducting retail pharmacy businesses, at their registered pharmacies.

Production. By reg. 5, licence holders may produce drugs in accordance with the terms and conditions of their licence at the premises in respect of which their names are entered, and in compliance with the conditions, supply or offer to supply sch. 1 drugs, provided that the recipient licences.

By reg. 9 (1) (c), persons whose names are in registers kept for the purpose by the Home Department may produce, at the premises in respect of which their names are entered, and in compliance with any conditions, sch. 3 drugs.

Supplying and Offering to Supply.

By reg. 5, licence holders may supply or offer to supply drugs in accordance with the terms and conditions of their licences.

By reg. 8 (2), practitioners, pharmacists, persons lawfully conducting retail pharmacy businesses, matrons of hospitals or nursing homes, hospital ward and theatre sisters, laboratory researchers, public analysts, sampling officers, testers, and Pharmaceutical Society inspectors may, when acting in their capacities, supply or offer to supply sch. 1 or 2 drugs. Persons whose names are entered in registers kept for the purposes by the Home Department may, under reg 8. (4), be entitled to possess the same.

By reg. 8 (5), ship owners and ship masters without a doctor on board, may supply sch. 1 or 2 drugs to the crew, or to any person who may lawfully supply the drug, or to a constable for destruction. Installation managers of offshore installations enjoy a like exemption.

The cultivation of cannabis is the subject of reg. 12. It may be cultivated only under licence from the Home Department. The smoking of cannabis or cannabis resin is, under reg. 13, permitted only on premises for the time being approved by the Home Department.

Documentation is the subject of the remaining Regulations.

By reg. 14, documents must be obtained by the supplier of controlled drugs from the recipient.

First, if the supplier is not a practitioner, and does not supply on a prescription, then if the person taking delivery purports to be sent by or on behalf of the person to whom the drug is to be supplied, (the recipient), and such person is not authorised by any provision of the Regulations to have the drugs in his possession (other than the authority of a person engaged in conveying the drug to a person authorised by the Regulations to have it in his possession), then no delivery is permitted unless that person (the recipient's messenger or agent) produces to the supplier a statement in writing signed by the recipient that he (the agent) is empowered to receive the drug.

Secondly, when the supplier supplies the drug, otherwise than on a prescription, or by way of administration to a practitioner, the matron of a hospital or nursing home, a laboratory researcher, a ship owner or ship master of a ship with no doctor, the master of a foreign ship in a U.K. port, or the installation manager of an offshore installation, then the supplier must obtain from the recipient a written requisition. This must be signed by the recipient, and contain specified details. When the recipient is a practitioner urgently requiring a controlled drug, and the supplier is satisfied there is an emergency, the delivery may be effected against an undertaking to furnish the requisition with 24 hours.

These provisions in reg. 14 do not apply to sch. 1 drugs, or to poppy-straw.

Regulation 15 lays down the form which a prescription must be in. Unless the drug is a sch. 1 drug, the prescription must:–
(1) be in indelible ink and signed by the issuer, and dated;
(2) be written by the practitioner in his own handwriting, so far as the patient's name and address and the dose are concerned;
(3) specify the address of the issuer, except in the case of a health prescription;
(4) have the words "for dental treatment only" if issued by a dentist, and the words "for dental treatment only" if issued by a veterinary practitioner;
(5) specify the patient's name and address, or that of the person taking delivery in the case of a veterinary surgeon's prescription;
(6) specify the dose to be taken, and if it is a preparation the strength, and in any other case the quantity;
(7) contain a direction specifying the amount of each instalment, if applicable, and the intervals.

In the case of hospitals and nursing homes, the prescriptions may be written on the patient's bed card or case sheet.

The prescription being now regularly issued, we come to reg. 16, and the duty of the chemist or pharmacist. He must see the prescription complies with reg. 15 above. The address of the practitioner must be in the U.K. The chemist or other supplier must be satisfied as to signature. He must not supply before, or later than thirteen weeks after, the date in the prescription. He must mark the date of dispensing, and except in the case of a health prescription, retain it.

Prescriptions issued for the purposes of a scheme for testing drugs are, by reg. 17, exempted from the provisions of regs. 15 and 16. Prescriptions under the Food and Drugs Acts issued to sampling officers are similarly exempted.

Bottles and containers must, by reg. 18, be marked. This does not apply to sch 1 drugs,or to poppy-straw, or to drugs supplied on a practitioner's prescription. The amount, dosage units, etc. must be shown.

By reg. 19, every supplier must keep a register. The entries must be in chronological sequence. Every quantity obtained, and supplied, must be shown. He must use a separate register for each class of drugs. Persons authorised by reg. 5, under licence from the Home Department, to supply drugs, are exempt from reg. 19. So are ward and theatre sisters in hospitals and nursing homes.

Regulation 20 says that every person required to keep a register under reg. 19 must comply with certain requirements.

The class of drugs must be specified at the head of the page.

Each entry must be made on the day the drug is obtained or supplied.

No cancellation, obliteration or alteration is to be made, except by marginal note or footnote.

Every entry and correction must be in indelible ink.

The register must be produced on demand to a person authorised by the Home Department, and the person keeping it shall on demand furnish particulars in respect of the obtaining or supplying by him of sch. 2 and 4 drugs, and produce the stock of drugs in his possession.

If the supplier carries on business at more than one set of premises, a separate register shall be kept in respect of each premises. Not more than one register shall be kept at one time in respect of each class of drugs. Each register must be kept at the premises to which it relates.

In the case of drugs in sch. 2 being supplied to a ship's crew, reg.

21 provides for entries in the log book, or alternatively a master's report.

Similarly, with offshore installations, the installation log book is to be used. Midwives obtaining and administering pethidine must make entries in books, giving the name and address of the supplier and also of the patient.

Regulation 23 concerns the preservation of records, relating to drugs in sch. 1. Every producer of drugs specified in sch. 1, and every wholesale dealer in such drugs, must keep invoices and other records and preserve them for two years, in respect of drugs obtained and drugs supplied. Retail dealers in sch. 1 drugs must do likewise in respect of drugs they obtain.

Regulation 24 deals with the destruction of controlled drugs. Persons required to keep records with respect to sch. 2 and 4 drugs must not destroy such drugs, or cause them to be destroyed, except in the presence of and in accordance with any directions given by an "authorised person", (an expression defined in the Regulation). Such person may take a sample of a drug to be destroyed for an analysis. The records kept must give particulars of the destruction, including the date. Masters and owners of ships, and installation managers of offshore installations, must not destroy sch. 2 drugs, but instead, if the drugs are no longer required, must dispose of the same to a constable, or a person who may lawfully supply sch. 2 drugs.

Regulation 25 contains transitional provisions.

By reg. 25 (1), a licence under S.6 of the 1965 Act, (the section which, repeating the 1964 Act, made it an offence to cultivate any cannabis plant except under licence), continued in force under the 1973 Regulations, for the same period of time as if the 1965 Act had not been repealed, and had effect as if it had been issued for the pruposes of reg. 12 (see ante) of the 1973 Regulations.

Licences under the Dangerous Drugs (No.2) Regulations 1964, in force before the repeal of the 1965 Act, similarly continued in force, and so did authorities granted in respect of any class of persons for the purposes of the 1964 Regulations, and in force before the repeal of the 1965 Act.

Registers, records, books, prescriptions and other documents required to be preserved under reg. 26 of the 1964 Regulations were, by reg. 25 of the 1973 Regulations, required to be preserved for the same time as if the 1965 Act had not been repealed.

For human administration, certain controlled drugs, e.g. morphine are pharmacy medicines, when within specified strengths. The maximum dose for morphine is 3 mg. The maximum strength for a solid dosage unit is 300 mcg. In regard to animal administration, any veterinary drug containing any controlled drug is a prescription only medicine. See the Medicines Act 1968, and also (inter alia) the Medicines (Prescription Only) Amendment (No.2) Order 1978, and the Medicines (Sale or Supply) (Miscellaneous Provisions) Amendment Regulations 1978.

X

Miscellaneous.   It remains to deal with the Misuse of Drugs (Safe Custody) Regulations 1973, (S.I. No. 798). These were made on April 19th, 1973. Regulations 1,2, and 5, and sch. 1, came into operation on July 1st, 1973. The remainder were intended to come into operation on October 1st, 1974. By the Misuse of Drugs (Safe Custody) (Amendment) Regulations 1974, the April 1st, 1975 was substituted in reg. 1 for the April 1st, 1974, (no doubt the change may have been connected with local government reorganisation or some industrial dispute or change of government).

The Regulations, with effect from July 1st, 1973, require controlled drugs other than those specified in sch. 1 generally to be kept either in a locked safe or room or in a locked receptacle.

The drugs specified and examples in sch. 1 are:–

1.   Any controlled drug specified in sch. 1 to the Misues of Drugs Regulations 1973.

2.   Any liquid preparation, designed for administration otherwise than by injection, which contains any of the following substances and products, i.e.

(a)Amphetamine; dexamphetamine; levamphetamine

(b)Benziphetamine

(c)Chlorphentermine

(d)Mephentermine

(e)Methaqualone

(f)Methylamphetamine

(g)Methylphenidate

(h)Phendimetrazine

(i)Phenmetrazine

(j)Pipradol

(k)Any stereoisomeric form of a substance specified in any of paras. (b) to (j) above.

(l)Any salt of a substance specified in any of paras. (a) to (k) above.

The Regulations require, with effect from April 1st, 1975, that where controlled drugs are kept on premises occupied by a retail pharmacist, or in a nursing home or similar institution, and are not under the supervision of a pharmacist or the person in charge, the drugs should be kept in a locked safe, cabinet or room which complies with the requirements of sch. 2 to the Regulations, or alternatively, in the case of a registered pharmacy, which is certified by the local chief officer of police as providing an adequate degree of security. Provision is made, by reg 4, in the latter case, for the inspection of premises by or on behalf of the chief officer of police for the area where the premises are, and the renewal and cancellation (renewal for a further year, and cancellation for breach of any condition in the certificate or any change of circumstances or the refusal of entry to a police officer), of certificate issued, following inspection, in respect of safes, cabinets and rooms.

So a doctor must, under reg. 5, keep his drugs in a receptacle, which can only be opened by him or a person he authorises, and turn the key. The chemist must, subject to reg 4, comply with the requirements of sch. 2, the rules in which demonstrate a passion for order, and are most technical.

The chemist commits an offence for example, if the safe or cabinet is not constructed in accordance with para. 2 of Sch. 2, or if the levers of the lock do not comply with the same paragraph. Walls of rooms must be of brick, concrete, steel mesh or sheet steel. Ceilings must be of solid concrete, or steel mesh or sheet steel. Doorway frames and glass windows have not escaped the draftsman's attention. Service hatches must be guarded by grilles of steel. There are 4½ pages of Sch. 2, setting out the detailed structural requirements.

When an order or a prescription for a controlled drug, or a preparation of a controlled drug, is given in the Imperial system, the equivalent metric amount has to be given as per the Weights and Measures (Equivalents for Dealing with Drugs) Regulations 1970.

Cumulative lists of additions and alterations to the classified lists and schedules, not only of controlled drugs, but of medicinal products and poisons as well, are published regularly in the *Pharmaceutical Journal,* to which the curious reader is referred.

As to licence fees, please see the Misuse of Drugs (Licence Fees) Regulations 1979, (S.I. No. 218). These Regulations became operative on April 1st, 1979.

With that, our book can end. Those interested in the pro-Cannabis and anti-Cannabis arguments are referred to M. Schofield's "The Strange Case of Pot", Penguin Books, 1969, and J.D.P. Graham's "Cannabis Now", H.M.M. Publishers, 1977, while to those who wish to read a thriller (incidentally based on fact) about the weird and wonderful machinations of the world's drug rings, and how they are rumbled at last, Detective Inspector Lee's "Operation Julie", 1978, can be recommended. Is the permissive society to blame? What do the public really think about controlled drugs? These questions, and more, need examination in a wide context, if all the causes and consequences are to be judges.

HOME OFFICE statistics on the number of persons found guilty of drug offences during the years 1973 to 1976 inclusive.

Type of Drug	1973	1974	1975	1976
Total found guilty of offences involving all drugs	14,439	12,137	11,603	12,482
Cocaine	186	394	402	335
Heroin	438	462	418	469
Methadone	357	487	513	423
Dipipanone	n/a	397	438	373
LSD	1,244	827	791	624
Cannabis	11,111	9,237	8,837	9,748
Amphetamine	1,750	1,503	1,525	1,901
Other drugs	n/a	n/a	1,653	1,291

Appendix B

EXTRACT from the Report of the Wootton Committee (1968). (Cannabis)

"In considering the scale of penalties our main aim, having regard to our view of the known effects of cannabis, is to remove for practical purposes, the prospect of imprisonment for possession of a small amount and to demonstrate that taking the drug in moderation is a relatively minor offence. For the forseeable future, our objection is clear: to bring about a situation in which it is extremely unlikely that anyone will go to prison for an offence involving only possession for personal use or for supply on a very limited scale."

"In its final report of November 1967, the Permanent Central Narcotics Board conceded: "The abuse of cannabis is more widespread than that of any substance under international control. It is also the substance about which for the time being the Board has the least information . . ." It repeated the caveat of 1965, namely that opposition to the control of cannabis was "contrary to the advice of scientific and medical authorities of international repute". It recalled that at the 1961 Plenipotentiary Convention, attended by 74 delegates, cannabis had been classified among particularly dangerous substances".

Appendix C

EXTRACT from the Canadian Le Dain Report (1972) Cannabis.

"The costs to a significant number of individuals, the majority of whom are young people, and to society generally, of a policy of prohibition of simple possession are not justified by the potential for harm of cannabis, and the additional influence which such a policy is likely to have upon perception of harm, demand and availability."

Appendix D

EXTRACT for the United States Shafter Report (1972). (Cannabis)

"Possession of herbal cannabis for personal use should no longer be an offence, but herbal cannabis possessed in public should remain contraband, subject to summary seizure and forfeiture. Casual distribution of small amounts of herbal cannabis for no remuneration or insignificant remuneration not involving profit, should no longer be an offence".

Appendix E

EXTRACT from the Report of the Working Party of the B.M.A. describing the effects of amphetamines (1968).

"Clinical picture

(i) Habitual consumption of amphetamines and amphetamine-like compounds in Britain is seen in two types of patient. Firstly, those often middle-aged women who have been prescribed tablets for slimming or for treatment of depression, and, having experienced a sense of euphoria and increased energy, stay on the drug; and, secondly, younger persons who take the drugs for 'kicks' to experience the 'high' and to stay awake at night and become 'hooked'.

(ii) Amphetamines are relatively non-toxic in the physical sense; if they were not so then drug abuse of the order now seen could not have occurred. Large doses of amphetamine which are fatal are usually the result of one of three processes: (a) combination with other drugs, (b) complications of intravenous injection such as septicaemia, bacterial endocardities, malaria, jaundice, or tetanus, or (c) suicide during the depression which may occur as the effects of the drug wear off.

(iii) The physical signs and symptoms of large doses of amphetamine include tachycardia, increased pulse pressure, cardiac arhythmia, and occasionally circulatory collapse. Cardiovascular symptoms are not so prominent in accounts of phenmetrazine intoxications.

(iv) Other effects include dilated pupils, nystagmus, and uncontrolled movements, which may take the form of head banging in small children. Reflexes are brisk, and ataxic movements have been described. Teeth-grinding and chewing movements are frequent and ulcers develop on the lips and tongue. Anorexia, dry mouth, and loss of weight are seen when large doses have been taken often continuously for a week. Thirst may be prominent, and with phenmetrazine an antipathy to alcohol is described, despite the thirst.

(v) The patients are often restless, irritable, and antisocial. Later rapid speech and verbal aggression are common, and overt aggression may occur. Involvement in crime is described, and accident proneness has been reported because overconfidence leads to lack of care and because of ataxia. Other patients describe a cleaning-up 'mania' or 'getting hung up' on an activity such as cleaning a wall, which they continue to do for hours.

Prepsychosis and Psychosis

(vi) Since the syndrome of psychosis due to amphetamines and amphetamine-like compounds has been widely recognized it has been possible to define a prepsychotic syndrome, which is, however, easy to miss in its early stages. The working party studied incidents due to amphetamine, dexamphetamine, Drinamyl, phenmetrazine, methylphenidate, and diethylpropion. The clinical picture may vary according to the patient's individual response to the drugs, the time of day they are taken, the conditions under which they are consumed, and, it seems likely, the characteristics of the individual drug, but the following characteristics have been identified: (a) the patient makes persistent demands for supplies, and his reasons for this request may seem bizarre or frankly false; (b) pursuance of the professional interview may precipitate an aggressive reaction, because of what appears to the patient to be a threat by the doctor to withhold what the patient regards as essential supplies; (c) irritability, over-activity, and sensitiveness to noise and frustration may be noted; and (d) it may be possible for the doctor to elicit this syndrome, but it may be clearly described by friends and relatives in terms of deterioration of mood or temperament.

(vii) The clinical picture may be confused by depression of two origins: (a) depression which was the original reason for the exhibition of a central nervous stimulant, and (b) depression on withdrawal of amphetamines. There is a risk of suicide at this stage, and the patient may turn to alcohol or sedatives or other drugs in an attempt to offset the withdraw effects. The popularity of Drinamyl, examphetamine, and amylobarbitone with patients would appear to be related to the fact that the barbiturates minimize both the excitability and the withdrawal depression following amphetamine. If Drinamyl has been given it should be withdrawn slowly, and perhaps phenytoin or other anticonvulsants prescribed, as barbiturate withdrawal occurs in non-epileptic patients.

(viii) The differential diagnosis of amphetamine psychosis from paranoid schizophrenia rests mainly on the prompt disappearance of the conditions on withdrawal of the amphetamines, usually in less than one week. Tests include the demonstration of amphetamines in the urine by chemical tests and chromatography. In patients with negative urine tests who do not improve, the possibility that the amphetamines have precipitated the onset of overt psychosis in latent schizophrenia should be considered.

(ix) No special treatment is necessary for an amphetamine psychosis other than drug withdrawal. It may be necessary to use phenothiazides in order to control the psychosis and restlessness. The onset of depression may bring a risk of suicide. Attention must be given to the social and psychological factors which have led to the drug abuse. Follow-up of patients is essential, as relapse is the rule rather than the exception if and when supplies of amphetamine becomes available. Some 6 to 12 months' aftercase may be required, and it seems likely that some cases will require continuous psychiatric supervision and treatment.

(x) To summarize, amphetamine and amphetamine-related compounds are probably capable of influencing every aspect of human behaviour, and amphetamine intoxication must be considered in the differential diagnosis of all cases of psychosis and many other organic and psychiatric syndromes. Amphetamines should be prescribed only after careful consideration of the personal and family history to ensure that the patient has a balanced personality."

Appendix F

EXTRACT from the Report by the Advisory Committee on Drug Dependence (The Amphetamines and LSD) (1970)

"Very small amounts may profoundly affect the mind: one-millionth of a gram or even less of the drug per kilogram body weight taken by mouth may have a considerable effect in this way, and of this dose only approximately one per cent penetrates the brain. The effects of a single dose of LSD are of three main kinds — autonomic, sensory and emotional. In general these begin to appear in that order, starting some 15-30 minutes after an oral dose. The effects may reach a peak between 2 and 6 hours later and last for 12 to 24 hours, sometimes longer. Tolerance, as shown by the mental effects is developed rapidly so that a dose taken within 1 or 2 days of the previous one is generally ineffective. This tolerance is not overcome at that time except by greatly increased amounts. It is, however, soon lost completely and a dose 5 or 6 days later usually produces the full effects. There is a cross-tolerance to mescaline and psilocybin and psilocin, but not to cannabis or amphetamine. This means that any person who has been indulging in cannabis or amphetamine will feel the full effects of a dose of LSD. Certain drugs in legitimate medical use increase the effect of LSD on the mind (for example reserpine) and others prevent it (e.g. mono amine oxidase inhibitors). Certain sedative drugs (e.g. phenothiazines) may cut short the psychotomimetic effects.

There are considerable qualitative differences between individual reactions, though these occur in a general framework that is largely specific to the drug. As with other drugs acting on the central nervous system these reflect in the personality, interests and social circumstances of the individual as well as his mood at the time that the drug is taken. Direct effects are exerted on the nervous system and may be attributable in part to interference with the role of the important naturally occurring chemical regulators serotonin and noradrenaline. LSD increases the amount of serotonin in the central nervous system and changes the pattern of its distribution in the brain cells; stores of noradrenaline, however, are depleted. Whatever the precise action, it results in two groups of obvious effects:

   (a)   disturbances of regulatory nervous systems, which resemble those of sympathetic over-activity. One or all of the following symptoms or effects may be present — loss of appetite, nausea, vomiting or diarrhoea, trembling, sweating, dilated pupils, rise or fall in blood pressure, rise in blood sugar level and temperature, goose flesh, quickened or slowed pulse and depressed breathing, enhancement or inhibition of reflexes, dizziness, interference with sleep, inco-ordination and shakiness (tremor), and

(b)   alteration of visual, and less commonly, auditory and other senses, plus distortion or loss of the sense of position in space, and of the body image, which may proceed to depersonalisation. Consequential disorders of thought and of the estimation of time may be associated with extreme alterations in mood. Hallucinations, in the strict sense, seldom occur, but the specific perpetual or sensory disturbances may be elaborated into a very complicated visual and emotional experience, difficult to record or communicate to others and rapidly changing. The tone of this may be aesthetic, sensuous or transcendental, and may oscillate slowly or rapidly between these qualities. The content of sexuality varies markedly. Some people describe predominantly orgiastic and euphoric experiences, others mainly mystical and ecstatic states. Amongst the latter some have been disappointed in not acquiring transcendental knowledge or a feeling of "oneness" as promised by enthusiasts. The effects, especially emotional, of the drug depend heavily on the situation in which it is taken, the expectations of the taker (and also on the attitudes communicated by the person who is giving the drug) his personality and background, and the social and cultural setting. Hence, no account of experience with LSD is so highly coloured and none so jejune as to be beyond credence. Most takers report both pleasant and unpleasant effects, and a predominantly pleasurable experience may change into the opposite within the same occasion or on successive occasions.

Psychological measurements during the period of LSD intoxication are difficult to perform since the subject is generally preoccupied with his own experiences. They generally fail to reflect the claim that the drug confers the power to resolve personal and intellectual problems.

Physical dependence does not occur but intense desire to continue use of the drug is quite frequently encountered, though almost as frequently denied by the user. Harmful mental states can occur. During the first few hours after taking the drug there may be violent behaviour; a panic-stricken or paranoid patient may attack others or he may hurt himself. Some users attempt to kill, or actually kill, themselves or others because they have apparently developed either a self-hatred or a feeling of superior power and invulnerability. Recrudescences, apparently without repeated experience of the drug, have been reported, sometimes separated by a period of several months. The causal relationship is, however, obviously difficult to establish in such cases.

In some subjects, lasting disturbances, depersonalisation, chronic dread, depression and mood swings and paranoid attitudes and beliefs, may be found following repeated exposure to LSD. The evidence does not suggest that all those suffering in this way were mentally unstable before they began taking the drug. Purchase of the drug through illicit channels may increase the possibility of such reactions because supplies obtained in this way may be impure; the exact dose is then very seldom known. Adolescents and young adults who are psychologically and socially unstable stand in the most danger of prolonged harmful reactions, but these may occur in some individuals of apparently good previous personality."

Appendix G

TEXT of the Misuse of Drugs Regulations 1973 (excluding the Schedules and the Transitional Provisions).

THE MISUSE OF DRUGS REGULATIONS 1973
ARRANGEMENT OF REGULATIONS

PART I

GENERAL
1. Citation and commencement.
2. Interpretation.
3. Metric system and imperial system.

PART II
EXEMPTIONS FROM CERTAIN PROVISIONS OF THE MISUSE OF DRUGS ACT 1971
4. Exceptions for drugs in sch. 1 and poppy-straw.
5. Licences to produce etc controlled drugs.
6. General authority to possess.

PART III

REQUIREMENTS AS TO DOCUMENTATION AND RECORD KEEPING

PART IV

MISCELLANEOUS

PART V

GENERAL

Citation and commencement

1. These Regulations may be cited as the Misuse of Drugs Regulations 1973 and shall come into operation on July 1, 1973.

Interpretation

2. (1) In these Regulations, unless the context otherwise requires,

the expression —

"the Act" means the Misuse of Drugs Act 1971;

"authorised as a member of a group" means authorised by virtue of being a member of a class respecting which the Secretary of State has granted an authority under and for the purposes of regs. 8(3), 9(3) or 10(3) which is in force, and "his group authority", in relation to a person who is a member of such a class, means the authority so granted to that class;

"health prescription" means a prescription issued by a doctor or a dentist either under the National Health Service Acts 1946 to 1973 the National Health Service (Scotland) Acts 1947 to 1973 the Health Services Act (Northern Ireland) 1971 or the National Health Service (Isle of Man) Act 1948 (an Act of Tynwald) or upon a form isued by a local authority for use in connection with the health service of that authority;

"installation manager" and "offshore installation" have the same meanings as in the Mineral Workings (Offshore Installations) Act 1971,

"master" has the same meaning as in the Merchant Shipping Act 1894;

"matron or acting matron" includes any male nurse occupying a similar position;

"the Merchant Shipping Acts" means the Merchant Shipping Acts 1894 to 1971;

"officer of customs and excise" means an officer within the meaning of the Customs and Excise Act 1952,

"prescription" means a prescription issued by a doctor for the medical treatment of a single individual, by a dentist for the dental treatment of a single individual or by a veterinary surgeon or veterinary practitioner for the purposes of animal treatment;

"register" means a bound book and does not include any form of loose leaf register or card index;

"registered pharmacy" has the same meaning as in the Medicines Act 1968;

"retail dealer" means a person lawfully conducting a retail pharmacy business or a pharmacist engaged in supplying drugs to the public at a health centre within the meaning of the Medicines Act 1968;

"sister or acting sister" includes any male nurse occupying a similar position;

"wholesale dealer" means a person who carries on the business of selling drugs to persons who buy to sell again.

(2) In these Regulations any reference to a Regulation or Schedule shall be construed as a reference to a Regulation contained in these Regulations or, as the case may be, to a Schedule thereto; and any reference in a Regulation or Schedule to a paragraph shall be construed as a reference to a paragraph of that Regulation or Schedule.

(3) In these Regulations any reference to any enactment shall be construed as a reference to that enactment as amended, and as including a reference thereto as extended or applied, by or under any other enactment.

(4)Nothing in these Regulations shall be construed as derogating from any power or immunity of the Crown, its servants or agents.

(5) The Interpretation Act 1889 shall apply for the interpretation of these Regulations as it applies for the interpretation of an Act of Parliament.

Metric system and imperial system
3.　(1) For the purposes of these Regulations —
　　(a) a controlled drug shall not be regarded as supplied otherwise than on a prescription or other order by reason only that the prescription or order specifies a quantity of the controlled drug in terms of the imperial system and the quantity supplied is the equivalent of that amount in the metric system;
　　(b) where any person may lawfully be in possession of a quantity of a controlled drug determined by or under these Regulations in terms of the imperial system he shall be deemed not to be in possession of a quantity of that controlled drug in excess of the first-mentioned quantity by reason only that he is in possession of a quantity of that drug which is the equivalent of the first-mentioned quantity in the metric system.
　　(2)　For the purposes of this Regulation the quantity of a controlled drug in the metric system which is the equivalent of a particular quantity in the imperial system shall be taken to be the appropriate quantity ascertained in accordance with the provisions of the Weights and Measures (Equivalents for dealing with drugs) Regulations 1970.

PART II

EXEMPTIONS FROM CERTAIN PROVISIONS OF THE MISUSE OF DRUGS ACT 1971

Exceptions for drugs in sch. 1 and poppy-straw

(1) Sections 3(1) and 5(1) of the Act (which prohibit the importation, exportation and possession of controlled drugs) shall not have effect in relation to the controlled drugs specified in sch. 1.

(2) Sections 4(1) (which prohibits the production and supply of controlled drugs) and 5(1) of the Act shall not have effect in relation to poppy-straw.

Licences to produce etc. controlled drugs

5. Where any person is authorised by a licence of the Secretary of State issued under this Regulation and for the time being in force to produce, supply, offer to supply or have in his possession any controlled drug, it shall not by virtue of s. 4(1) or 5(1) of the Act be unlawful for that person to produce, supply, offer to supply or have in his possession that drug in accordance with the terms of the licence and in compliance with any conditions attached to the licence.

General authority to possess

6. Any of the following persons may, notwithstanding the provision of s. 5(1) of the Act, have any controlled drug in his possession, that is to say —

(a) a constable when acting in the course of his duty as such;

(b) a person engaged in the business of a carrier when acting in the course on that business;

(c) a person engaged in the business of the Post Office when acting in the course of that business;

(d) an officer of customs and excise when acting in the course of his duty as such;

(e) a person engaged in the work of any laboratory to which the drug has been sent for forensic examination when acting in the course of his duty as a person so engaged;

(f) a person engaged in conveying the drug to a person authorised by these Regulations to have it in his possession.

Administration of drugs in schs. 1, 2 and 3

7. (1) Any person may administer to another any drug specified in sch. 1.

(2) A doctor or dentist may administer to a patient any drug

specified in sch. 2 or 3.

(3) Any person other than a doctor or dentist may administer to a patient, in accordance with the directions of a doctor or dentist, any drug specified in sch. 2 or 3.

Production and supply of drugs in schs. 1 and 2

(1) Notwithstanding the provisions of s. 4(1)(a) of the Act:

(a) a practitioner or pharmacist, acting in his capacity as such, may manufacture or compound any drug specified in sch. 1 or 2;

(b) a person lawfully conducting a retail pharmacy business and acting in his capacity as such may, at the registered pharmacy at which he carries on that business, manufacture or compound any drug specified in sch. 1 or 2.

(2) Notwithstanding the provisions of s. 4(1)(b) of the Act any of the following persons, that is to say:—

(a) a practitioner;

(b) a pharmacist;

(c) a person lawfully conducting a retail pharmacy business;

(d) the matron or acting matron of a hospital or nursing home which is wholly or mainly maintained by a public authority out of public funds or by a charity or by voluntary subscriptions;

(e) in the case of such a drug supplied to her by a person responsible for the dispensing and supply of medicines at the hospital or nursing home, the sister or acting sister for the time being in charge of a ward, theatre or other department in such a hospital or nursing home as aforesaid;

(f) a person who is in charge of a laboratory the recognized activities of which consist in, or include, the conduct of scientific education or research and which is attached to a university, university college or such a hospital as aforesaid or to any other institution approved for the purpose by the Secretary of State;

(g) a public analyst appointed under s. 89 of the Food and Drugs Act 1955 or s. 27 of the Food and Drugs (Scotland) Act 1956;

(i) A sampling officer within the meaning of sch. 3 to the Medicines Act 1968;

(j) a person employed or engaged in connection with a scheme for testing the quality or amount of the drugs, preparations and appliances supplied under the National Health Service Acts 1946 to 1973 or the National Health Service (Scotland) Acts 1947 to 1973 and the Regulations made thereunder;

(k) an inspector appointed by the Pharmaceutical Society of Great Britain under s. 25 of the Pharmacy and Poisons Act 1933, may, when acting in his capacity as such, supply or offer to supply any drug specified in sch. 1 or 2 to any person who may lawfully have that drug in his possession:

Provided that nothing in this paragraph authorises —

(i) the matron or acting matron of a hospital or nursing home, having a pharmacist responsible for the dispensing and supply of medicines, to supply or offer to supply any drug;

(ii) a sister or acting sister for the time being in charge of a ward, theatre or other department to supply any drug otherwise than for administration to a patient in that ward, theatre or department in accordance with the directions of a doctor or dentist.

(3) Notwithstanding the provisions of s. 4(1)(b) of the Act, a person who is authorised as a member of a group may, under and in accordance with the terms of his group authority and in compliance with any conditions attached thereto, supply or offer to supply any drug specified in sch. 1 or 2 to any person who may lawfully have that drug in his possession.

(4) Notwithstanding the provisions of s. 4(1)(b) of the Act, a person whose name is for the time being entered in the register kept for the purposes of this paragraph by the Secretary of State may, at the premises in respect of which his name is so entered and in compliance with any conditions subject to which his name is so entered, supply or offer to supply any drug specified in sch. 1 to any person who may lawfully have that drug in his possession.

(5) Notwithstanding the provisions of s. 4(1)(b) of the Act —

(a) the owner of a ship, or the master of a ship which does not carry a doctor on board as part of her complement, may supply or suffer to supply any drug specified in sch. 1 or 2 —

(i) to any member of the crew;

(ii) to any person who may lawfully supply that drug; or

(iii) to any constable for the purpose of destruction;

(b) the installation manager of an offshore installation may supply or offer to supply any drug specified in sch. 1 or 2.

  (i) to any person on that installation, whether present in the course of his employment or not;
  (ii) to any person who may lawfully supply that drug; or
  (iii) to any constable for the purpose of destruction.

Production and supply of drugs in sch.3

9. (1) Notwithstanding the provisions of s. 4(1)(a) of the Act —

  (a) a practitioner or pharmacist, acting in his capacity as such, may manufacture or compound any drug specified in sch. 3;
  (b) a person lawfully conducting a retail pharmacy business and acting in his capacity as such may, at the registered pharmacy at which he carried on that business, manufacture or compound any drug specified in sch. 3;
  (c) a person whose name is for the time being entered in the register kept for the purpose of this sub-paragraph by the Secretary of State may produce, at the premises in respect of which his name is so entered and in compliance with any conditions subject to which his name is so entered, any drug specified in sch. 3.

  (2) Not withstanding the provisions of s. 4(1)(b) of the Act, any of the following persons, that is to say —

  (a) a practitioner;
  (b) a pharmacist;
  (c) a person lawfully conducting a retail pharmacy business;
  (d) the matron or acting matron of a hospital or nursing home;
  (e) in the case of such a drug supplied to her by a person responsible for the dispensing and supply of medicines at the hospital or nursing home, the sister or acting sister for the time being in charge of a ward, theatre or other department in a hospital or nursing home;
  (f) a person who is in charge of a laboratory the recognized activities of which consist in, or include, the conduct of scintific education or research;
  (g) a public analyst appointed under s. 89 of the Food and Drugs Act 1955 or s. 27 of the Food and Drugs (Scotland) Act 1956;
  (h) a sampling officer within the meaning of the Food and Drugs Act 1955 or the Food and Drugs (Scotland) Act

1965;

(i) a sampling officer within the meaning of sch. 3 to the Medicines Act 1968;

(j) a person employed or engaged in connection with a scheme for testing the quality or amount of the drugs, preparations and appliances supplied under the National Health Service Acts 1946 and 1973 or the National Health Service (Scotland) Acts 1947 and 1973 and the Regulations made thereunder;

(k) an inspector appointed by the Pharmaceutical Society of Great Britain under s. 25 of the Pharmacy and Poisons Act, 1933, may, when acting in his capacity as such, supply or offer to supply any drug specified in sch. 3 to any person who may lawfully have that drug in his possesson:

Provided that nothing in this paragraph authorises —

(i) the matron or acting matron of a hospital or nursing home having a pharmacist responsible for the dispensing and supply of medicines, to supply or offer to supply any drug;

(ii) a sister or acting sister for the time being in charge of a ward, theatre of other department to supply any drug otherwise than for administration to a patient in that ward, theatre or department in accordance with the directions of a doctor or dentist.

(3) Notwithstanding the provisions of s. 4(1)(b) of the Act, a person who is authorised as a member of a group may, under and in accordance with the terms of his group authority and in compliance with any conditions attached thereto, supply or offer to supply any drug specified in sch. 3 to any person who may lawfully have that drug in his possession.

(4) Nothwithstanding the provisions of s. 4(1)(b) of the Act —

(a) a person whose name is for the time being entered in the register kept for the purposes of this sub-paragraph by the Secretary of State may, at the premises in respect of which his name is so entered and in compliance with any conditions subject to which his name is so entered, supply or offer to supply any drug specified in sch. 3 to any person who may lawfully have that drug in his possession;

(b) a person whose name is for the time being entered in the register kept for the purposes of para. 1(c) by the Secretary of State may supply or offer any drug which he may, by virtue of his name being so entered, lawfully produce to any person who may lawfully have that drug in his possession.

(5) Notwithstanding the provisions of s. 4(1)(b) of the Act —

   (a) the owner of a ship, or the master of a ship which does not carry a doctor on board as part of her complement, may supply or offer to supply any drug specified in sch. 3 —

      (i) to any member of the crew; or

      (ii) to any person who may lawfully supply that drug;

   (b) the installation manager of an offshore installation may supply or offer to supply any drug specified in sch. 3 —

      (i) to any person on that installation, whether present in the course of his employment or not; or

      (ii) to any person who may lawfully supply that drug.

Possession of drugs in Schs. 2 and 3

10.   (1) Notwithstanding the provisions of s.5(1) of the Act —

   (a) a person specified in reg. 8(2) may have in his possession any drug specified in sch. 2;

   (b) a person specified in reg. 9(2) may have in his possession any drug specified in sch. 3,

for the purpose of acting in his capacity as such.

    (2) Notwithstanding the provisions of s. 5(1) of the Act a person

may have in his possession any drug specified in sch. 2 or 3 for administration for medical, dental or veterinary purposes in accordance with the directions of a practitioner:

Provided that this paragraph shall not have effect in the case of a person to whom the drug has been supplied by or on the prescription of a doctor if —

   (a) that person was then being supplied with any controlled drug by or on the prescription of another doctor and failed to disclose that fact to the first mentioned doctor before the supply by him or on his prescription; or

   (b) that person or any other person on his behalf made a declaration or statement, which was false in any particular, for the purpose of obtaining the supply or prescription.

    (3) Notwithstanding the provisions of s. 5(1) of the Act, a person who is authorised as a member of a group may, under and in accordance with the terms of his group authority and in compliance with any condictions attached thereto, have any drug specified in sch. 2 or 3 in his possession.

    (4) Notwithstanding the provisions of s. 5(1) of the Act —

   (a) a person whose name is for the time being entered in the register kept for the purposes of this sub-paragragh by the

Secretary of State may, in compliance with any conditions subject to which his name is so entered, have in his possession any drug specified in sch. 3;

(b) a person whose name is for the time being entered in the register kept for the purposes of reg. 9(1)(c) by the Secretary of State may have in his possession any drug which he may, by virtue of his name being so entered, lawfully produce;

(c) a person whose name is for the time being entered in the register kept for the purposes of reg. 9(4)(a) by the Secretary of State may have in his possession any drug which he may, by virtue of his name being so entered, lawfully supply or offer to supply.

(5) Notwithstanding the provisions of s. 5(1) of the Act —

(a) the owner of a ship, or the master of a ship which does not carry a doctor on board as part of her complement, may have in his possession any drug specified in sch. 2 or 3 so far as necessary for the purpose of compliance with the Merchant Shipping Acts;

(b) the master of a foreign ship which is in a port in Great Britain may have in his possession any drug specified in sch. 2 or 3 so far as necessary for the equipment of the ship;

(c) the installation manager of an offshore installation may have in his possession any drug specified in sch. 2 or 3 so far as necessary for the purpose of compliance with the Mineral Workings (Offshore Installations) Act 1971.

Exemption for midwives in respect of pethidine

11. (1) Notwithstanding the provisions of s. 4(1)(b) and 5(1) of the Act, a certified midwife, who has in accordance with the provisions of the Midwives Act 1951, or the Midwives (Scotland) Act 1951 notified to the local supervising authority her intention to practise, may, subject to the provisions of this Regulation —

(a) so far as necessary for the practice of her profession or employment as a midwife, have pethidine in her possession;

(b) so far as necessary as aforesaid, administer pethidine; and

(c) surrender to the appropriate medical officer any stocks of pethidine in her possession which are no longer required by her.

(2) Nothing in para. (1) authorises a midwife to have in her possession pethidine which has been obtained otherwise

than on a midwife's supply order signed by the appropriate medical officer.

(3) In this Regulation, the expression —
"appropriate medical officer" means —

(a) a doctor who is for the time being authorised in writing for the purpose of this Regulation by the local supervising authority for the region or area in which the pethidine was, or is to be, obtained; or

(b) for the purposes of para. (2), a person appointed under s. 17 of the Midwives Act 1951, or, as the case may be, s. 18 of the Midwives (Scotland) Act 1951, by that authority to exercise supervision over certified midwives within their area, who is for the time being authorised as aforesaid;

"certified midwife" and "local supervising authority" have the same meanings as in the Midwives Act 1951 or, in Scotland, the Midwives (Scotland) Act 1951; (as amended by the National Health Service Reorganisation Act 1974 and the National Health Service (Scotland) Act 1972 respectively)

"midwife's supply order" means an order in writing specifying the name and occupation of the midwife obtaining the pethidine, the purpose for which it is required and the total quantity to be obtained.

Cultivation under licence of Cannabis plant

12.   Where any person is authorised by a licence of the Secretary of State issued under this Regulation and for the time being in force to cultivate plants of the genus Cannabis, it shall not by virtue of s.6 of the Act be unlawful for that person to cultivate any such plant in accordance with the terms of the licence and in compliance with any conditions attached to the licence.

Approval of premises for cannabis smoking for research purposes.

13.   S.8 of the Act (which makes it an offence for the occupier of premises to permit certain activities there) shall not have effect in relation to the smoking of cannabis or cannabis resin for all the purposes of research on any premises for the time being approved for the purpose by the Secretary of State.

PART III

REQUIREMENTS AS TO DOCUMENTATION AND RECORD KEEPING

Documents to be obtained by supplier of controlled drugs

14. (1) Where a person (hereafter in this paragraph referred to as "the supplier") not being a practitioner, supplies a controlled drug otherwise than on a prescription, the supplier shall not deliver the drug to a person who —

(a) purports to be sent by or on behalf of the person to whom it is supplied (hereafter in this paragraph referred to as "the recipient"); and

(b) is not authorised by any provision of these Regulations other than the provisions of reg. 6(f) to have that drug in his possession,

unless that person produces to the supplier a statement in writing signed by the recipient to the effect that he is empowered by the recipient to receive that drug on behalf of the recipient, and the supplier is reasonably satisfied that the document is a genuine document.

(2) Where a person (hereafter in the paragraph referred to as "the supplier") supplies a controlled drug, otherwise than on a prescription or by way of administration, to any of the persons specified in para. (4), the supplier shall not deliver the drug —

(a) until he has obtained a requisition in writing which —

(i) is signed by the person to whom the drug is supplied (hereafter in this paragraph referred to as "the recipient");

(ii) states the name, address and profession or occupation of the recipient;

(iii) specifies the purpose for which the drug supplied is required and the total quantity to be supplied; and

(iv) where appropriate, satisfies the requirements of paragraph (5);

(b) unless he is reasonably satisfied that the signature is that of the person purporting to have signed the requisition and that that person is engaged in the profession or occupation specified in the requisition:

Provided that where the recipient is a practitioner and he represents that he urgently requires a controlled drug for the purpose of his profession, the supplier may, if he is reasonably satisfied that the recipient so requires the drug and is, by reason of some emergency, unable before delivery to furnish to the supplier a requisition in writing duly signed, deliver the drug to the recipient on an undertaking by the recipient to furnish such a requisition within the twenty-four hours next following.

(3) A person who has given such an undertaking as aforesaid shall deliver to the person by whom the controlled drug was supplied a signed requisition in accordance with the undertaking.

(4) The persons referred to in para. (2) are —
   (a) a practitioner;
   (b) the matron or acting matron of a hospital or nursing home;
   (c) a person who is in charge of a laboratory the recognized activities of which consist in, or include, the conduct of scientific education or research;
   (d) the owner of a ship, or the master of a ship which does not carry a doctor on board as part of her complement;
   (e) the master of a foreign ship in a port in Great Britain;
   (f) the installation manager of an offshore installation.

(5) A requisition furnished for the purposes of para. (2) shall —
   (a) where furnished by the matron or acting matron of a hospital or nursing home, be signed by a doctor or dentist employed or engaged in that hospital or nursing home;
   (b) where furnished by the master of a foreign ship, contain a statement, signed by the proper officer of the port health authority, or, in Scotland, the medical officer designated under s.21 of National Health Service (Scotland) Act 1972 by the Health Board, within whose jurisdiction the ship is, that the quantity of the drug to be supplied is the quantity necessary for the equipment of the ship.

(6) Where the person responsible for the dispensing and supply of medicines at any hospital or nursing home supplies a controlled drug to the sister or acting sister for the time being in charge of any ward, theatre or other department in that hospital or nursing home (hereafter in this paragraph referred to as "the recipient") he shall —
   (a) obtain a requisition in writing, signed by the recipient, which specifies the total quantity of the drug to be supplied; and
   (b) mark the requisition in such manner as to show that it has been complied with,

and any requisition obtained for the purposes of this paragraph shall be retained in the dispensary at which the drug was supplied and a copy of the requisition or a note of it shall be retained or kept by the recipient.

(7) Nothing in this Regulation shall have effect in relation to the drugs specified in sch. 1 or poppy-straw.

Forms of prescriptions

15. (1) Subject to the provisions of this Regulation, a person shall not issue a prescription containing a controlled drug other than a drug specified in sch. 1 unless the prescription complies with the following requirements, that is to say, it shall —

- (a) be in ink or otherwise so as to be indelible and be signed by the person issuing it with his usual signature and dated by him;
- (b) insofar as it specifies the information required by sub-paras. (e) and (f) below to be specified, be written by the person issuing it in his own handwriting;
- (c) except in the case of a health prescription, specify the address of the person issuing it;
- (d) have written thereon, if issued by a dentist, the words "for dental treatment only" and, if issued by a veterinary surgeon or a veterinary practitioner, the words "for animal treatment only";
- (e) specify the name and address of the person for whose treatment it is issued or, if it is issued by a veterinary surgeon or veterinary practitioner, of the person to whom the controlled drug prescribed is to be delivered;
- (f) specify the dose to be taken and —
  - (i) in the case of a prescription containing a controlled drug which is a preparation, the form and, where appropriate, the strength of the preparation, and either the total quantity (in both words and figures) of the preparation or the number (in both words and figures) of dosage units, as appropriate, to be supplied;
  - (ii) in any other case, the total quantity (in both words and figures) of the controlled drug to be supplied;
- (g) in the case of a prescription for a total quantity intended to be dispensed by instalments, contain a direction specifying the amount of the instalments of the total amount which may be dispensed and the intervals to be observed when dispensing.

(2) Paragraph 1(b) shall not have effect in relation to a prescription issued by a person approved (whether personally or as a member of a class) for the purposes of this paragraph by the Secretary of State.

(3) In the case of a prescription issued for the treatment of a patient in a hospital or nursing home, it shall be a sufficient compliance with para. 1(e) if the prescription is written on the patient's bed card or case sheet.

Provisions as to supply on prescription

16. (1) A person shall not supply a controlled drug other than a drug specified in sch. 1 on a prescription —
  (a) unless the prescription complies with the provisions of reg. 15;
  (b) unless the address specified in the prescription as the address of the person issuing it is an address within the United Kingdom;
  (c) unless he either is acquainted with the signature of the person by whom it purports to be issued and has no reason to suppose that it is not genuine, or has taken reasonably sufficient steps to satisfy himself that it is genuine;
  (d) before the date speficied in the prescription;
  (e) subject to para. (3), later than thirteen weeks after the date specified in the prescription.

(2) Subject to para. (3), a person dispensing a prescription containing a controlled drug other than a drug specified in sch. 1 shall, at the time of dispensing it, mark thereon the date on which it is dispensed and, unless it is a health prescription, shall retain it on the premises on which it was dispensed.

(3) In the case of a prescription containing a controlled drug other than a drug specified in sch. 1, which contains a direction that specified instalments of the total amount may be dispensed at stated intervals, the person dispensing it shall not supply the drug otherwise than in accordance with that direction and —
  (a) paragraph (1) shall have effect as if for the requirement contained in sub-para. (e) thereof there were substituted a requirement that the occasion on which the first instalment is dispensed shall not be later than thirteen weeks after the date specified in the prescription;
  (b) para. (2) shall have effect as if for the words "at the time of dispensing it" there were substituted the words "on each occasion on which an instalment is dispensed"

Exemption for certain prescriptions

17. Nothing in regs. 15 and 16 shall have effect in relation to a prescription issued for the purposes of a scheme for testing the quality and amount of the drugs, preparations and appliances supplied under the National Health Service Acts 1946 to 1973 or the National Health Service (Scotland) Acts 1947 to 1973 and the Regulations made thereunder or to any prescriptions issued for the purposes of the Food and Drugs Act 1955 or, in Scotland, the Food and Drugs (Scotland) Act 1956 to a sampling officer within the meaning of those Acts or for the purposes of the Medicines Act 1968 to a sampling officer within the meaning of that Act.

Marking of bottles and other containers

18. (1) Subject to para. (2), no person shall supply a controlled drug otherwise than in a bottle, package or other container which is plainly marked —

    (a) in the case of a controlled drug other than a preparation, with the amount of the drug contained therein;

    (b) in the case of a controlled drug which is a preparation —

        (i) made up into tablets, capsules or other dosage units, with the amount of each component (being a controlled drug) of the preparation in each dosage unit and the number of dosage units in the bottle, package or other container;

        (ii) not made up as aforesaid, with the total amount of the preparation in the bottle, package or other container and the percentage of each of its components which is a controlled drug.

(2) Nothing in this Regulation shall have effect in relation to the drugs specified in sch. 1 or poppy-straw or in relation to the supply of a controlled drug by or on the prescription of a practitioner.

Keeping of registers

19. (1) Subject to para. (3) and reg. 21, every person authorised by or under reg. 5 or 8 to supply any drug specified in sch. 2 or 4 shall comply with the following requirements, that is to say —

    (a) he shall, in accordance with the provisions of this Regulation and of reg. 20, keep a register and shall enter therein in chronological sequence in the form specified in Part I or Part II of sch. 5, as the case may require, particulars of every quantity of a drug specified in sch. 2 or 4 obtained by him and of every quantity of such a drug supplied (whether by way of administration or otherwise) by him whether to persons within or outside Great Britain;

(b) he shall use a separate register or separate part of the register for entries made in respect of each class of drugs, and each of the drugs specified in paras. 1, 3 and 6 of sch. 2 and paras. 1 and 3 of sch. 4 together with its salts and any preparation or other product containing it or any of its salts shall be treated as a separate class, so however that any stereoisomeric form of a drug or its salts shall be classed with that drug.

(2) Nothing in para. (1) shall be taken as preventing the use of a separate section within a register or separate part of a register in respect of different drugs or strengths of drugs comprised within the class of drugs to which that register or separate part relates.

(3) The foregoing provisions of this Regulation shall not have effect in relation to —

(a) a person licensed under reg. 5 to supply any drug, where the licence so directs; or

(b) the sister or acting sister for the time being in charge of a ward, theatre or other department in a hospital or nursing home.

Requirements as to registers

20.   Any person required to keep a register under reg. 19 shall comply with the following requirements, that is to say —

(a) the class of drugs to which the entries on any page of any such register relate shall be specified at the head of that page;

(b) every entry required to be made under reg. 19 in such a register shall be made on the day on which the drug is obtained or, as the case may be, on which the transaction in respect of the supply of the drug by the person required to make the entry takes place or, if that is not reasonably practicable, on the day next following that day;

(c) no cancellation, obliteration or alteration of any such entry shall be made, and a correction of such an entry shall be made only by way of marginal note or footnote which shall specify the date on which the correction is made;

(d) every such entry and every correction of such an entry shall be made in ink or otherwise so as to be indelible;

(e) such a register shall not be used for any purpose other than the purposes of these Regulations;

(f) the person so required to keep such a register shall on demand made by the Secretary of State or by any person authorised in writing by the Secretary of State in that behalf —

    (i) furnish such particulars as may be requested in respect of the obtaining or supplying by him of any drug specified in sch. 2 or 4, or in respect of any stock of such drugs in his possession;

    (ii) for the purpose of confirming any such particulars, produce any stock of such drugs in his possession;

    (iii) produce the said register and such other books or documents in his possession relating to any dealings in drugs specified in sch. 2 or 4 as may be requested;

(g) a separate register shall be kept in respect of each premises at which the person required to keep the register carries on his business or occupation but subject to that not more than one register shall be kept at one time in respect of each class of drug in respect of which he is required to keep a separate register, so, however, that a separate register may, with the approval of the Secretary of State, be kept in respect of each department of the business carried on by him;

(h) every such register in which entries are currently being made shall be kept at the premises to which it relates.

Record-keeping requirements in particular cases

21.   (1) Where a drug specified in sch. 2 is supplied in accordance with reg. 8(5)(a)(i) to a member of the crew of a ship, an entry in the official log book required to be kept under the Merchant Shipping Acts or, in the case of a ship which is not required to carry such an official log book, a report signed by the master of the ship, shall, notwithstanding anything in these Regulations, be a sufficient record of the supply if the entry or report specifies the drug supplied and, in the case of a report, it is delivered as soon as may be to the superintendent of a mercantile marine office established and maintained under the Merchant Shipping Acts.

(2) Where a drug specified in sch. 2 is supplied in accordance with reg. 8(5)(b)(i) to a person on an offshore installation, an entry in the installation log book required to be maintained under the Offshore Installation (Logbooks and Registration of Death) Regulations 1972 which specifies the drug supplied shall, notwithstanding anything in these Regulations, be a sufficient record of the supply.

(3) A midwife authorised by reg. 11(1) to have pethidine in her possession shall —

    (a) on each occasion on which she obtains a supply of pethidine, enter in a book kept by her and used solely for the purposes of this paragraph the date, the name and address of the person from whom the drug was obtained, the amount obtained and the form in which it was obtained; and

    (b) on administering pethidine to a patient, enter in the said book as soon as practicable the name and address of the patient, the amount administered and the form in which it was administered.

Preservation of registers, books and other documents

22.   (1) All registers and books kept in pursuance of reg. 19 or 21(3) shall be preserved for a period of two years from the date on which the last entry therein is made.

(2) Every requisition, order or prescription (other than a health prescription) on which a controlled drug is supplied in pursuance of these Regulations shall be preserved for a period of two years from the date on which the last delivery under it was made.

Preservation of records relating to drugs in sch. 1

23.   (1) A producer of any drug specified in sch. 1 and a wholesale dealer in any such drugs shall keep every invoice or other like record issued in respect of each quantity of such a drug obtained by him and in respect of each quantity of such a drug supplied by him.

(2) A retail dealer in any drug specified in sch. 1 shall keep every invoice or other like record issued in respect of each quantity of such a drug obtained by him.

(3) Every document kept in pursuance of this Regulation shall be preserved for a period of two years from the date on which it is issued:

    Provided that the keeping of a copy of the document made at any time during the said period of two years shall be treated for the purposes of this paragraph as if it were the keeping of the original document.

PART IV

MISCELLANEOUS

Destruction of controlled drugs

24.   (1) No person who is required by any provisions of, or by any term or condition of a licence having effect under, these Regulations to keep records with respect to a drug specified in sch. 2 or 4 shall destroy such a drug or cause such a drug to be destroyed except in the presence of and in accordance with any directions given by a person authorised (whether personally or as a member of a class) for the purposes of this paragraph by the Secretary of State (hereafter in the Regulation referred to as an "authorised person").

(2) An authorised person may, for the purpose of analysis, take a sample of a drug specified in sch. 2 or 4 which is to be destroyed.

(3) Where a drug specified in sch. 2 or 4 is destroyed in pursuance of para. (1) by or at the instance of a person who is required by any provision of, or by any term or condition of a licence under, these Regulations to keep a record in respect of the obtaining or supply of that drug, that record shall include particulars of the date of destruction and the quantity destroyed and shall be signed by the authorised person in whose presence the drug is destroyed.

(4) Where the master or owner of a ship or installation manager of an offshore installation has in his possession a drug specified in sch. 2 which he no longer requires, he shall not destroy the drug or cause it to be destroyed but shall dispose of it to a constable or to a person who may lawfully supply it.

APPENDIX H
FORM OF TWO SEARCH WARRANTS UNDER
THE MISUSE OF DRUGS ACT 1971.

(1)   IN the County/Petty Sessional Division of

To each and all the constables of the   Police Force.

I, the undersigned, sitting at the
Magistrates Court, am satisfied by information on oath that
there is reasonable ground for suspecting that controlled drugs
to which the Misuse of Drugs Act 1971 applies are, in
contravention of the Act or any regulations made thereunder,
in the possession of a person on premises in the police area at
(premises)

You are therefore authorised at any time or times within one
month from the date of this warrant to enter, if need be by
force, and to search the said premises and any persons found
therein and, if there is reasonable ground for suspecting that an
offence against the Act has been committed in relation to any
controlled drugs which may be found on the premises or in the
possession of any such person, to seize and detain those drugs.

Dated the   day of   197

Justice of the Peace for the County/Petty Sessional
Division first above mentioned.

SEARCH WARRANT
CONTROLLED DRUGS
Misuse of Drugs
Act 1971, s.23(3)(a)

(2)   IN the County/Petty Sessional Division of
To each and all the constables of the   Police Force.

I, the undersigned, sitting at the
Magistrates' Court, am satisfied by information on oath that
there is reasonable ground for suspecting that a document
which directly or indirectly relates to, or is connected with, a
transaction or dealing which would

(a) if carried out be an offence under the Act: or

(b)   if carried out or intended to be carried out in a place outside
the United Kingdom, be an offence against the provisions
of a corresponding law in force in that place,

is in the possession of a person on premises in the police area at
(premises)

You are therefore authorised at any time or times within one
month from the date of this warrant to enter, if need be by
force, and to search the said premises and any persons found
therein, and, if there is reasonable ground for suspecting that a
document found on the premises or in the possession of any
persons found therein is such a document as is mentioned
above, to seize and detain that document.

Dated the   day of   197

Justice of the Peace for the County/Petty Sessional
Division first above mentioned.

SEARCH WARRANT
DOCUMENT RELATING TO DRUG OFFENCE
Misuse of Drugs
Act 1971, s.23(3)(b).

THE PROCEEDS OF CRIME

The decision of the House of Lords in the case of Cuthbertson quashing the order of forfeiture in the "Operation Julie" case reveals a predictable, but glaring gap in the powers of the court to deal adequately with those who commit serious offences. The Howard League is accordingly to be congratulated for setting up a committee on the forfeiture of criminal property to examine this question and make recommendations. The League believes that one of the significant ways of gaining public acceptance for shorter prison sentences for non-violent offenders is to ensure that offenders disgorge the ill-gotten gains of their crime. The Committee will comprise Martin Iredale, N. Anthony Leifer, Clive Soley M.P., Christopher Staughton Q.C. and Prof. Nigel Walker C.B.E. Its secretary will be Andrew G.L. Nicol and its chairman the Hon. Mr. Justice Hodgson, formerly a member of the Law Commission and of the Butler Committee. Its terms of reference are "to consider the present law relating to the forfeiture of property associated with crime in the light of the House of Lords judgment in R. v Cutherbertson and Others, June 12, 1980; to consider the law relating to compensation and restitution of property to the victims of crime, and the operation of criminal bankruptcy; to assess how far the powers of criminal courts to impose monetary penalties meet the need to strip offenders of their ill-gotten gains; and whether further provisions are necessary to ensure that the fruits of crime are returned either to the innocent owners of the property or to the Crown. Communications to the Committee should be addressed to The Howard League for Penal Reform, 169 Clapham Road, London SW9 0PU.

SUBJECT INDEX

This index deals with the law generally applicable to all drugs and therefore omits most individual names. They are however catalogued by classes in the four schedules reproduced on pp. 20-5, (the classes) 46, 48-53, the commonest also being under the entry for drugs.